# How to Watch Birds

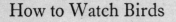

With *Where to Watch Birds*, his first b[...] an immediate success. He left a career as a teacher and lecturer at a college of education to become editor of the nine-volume encyclopedia, *Birds of the World*. In 1970 he took two months off on a Churchill Fellowship to study migration through North Africa. Subsequently he launched his own magazine *World of Birds*, but left after a year to write television scripts for Anglia Television's *Survival* series and to edit the company's house magazine, *The World of Survival*. He now devotes his time to full-time writing about birds and natural history. He lives in London, where his wife runs the wildlife photographic agency, Ardea. They have two children and a cottage in Sussex, where bird-watching and the family come first.

Also by John Gooders in Pan Books
Where to Watch Birds

John Gooders

# How to Watch Birds

illustrated by David Thelwell

First published 1975 by André Deutsch Limited
This edition published 1977 by Pan Books Ltd,
Cavaye Place, London SW10 9PG
© John Gooders 1975
ISBN 0 330 25029 9
Printed and bound in Great Britain by
Richard Clay (The Chaucer Press) Ltd, Bungay, Suffolk

To Timothy and Sophie
with the hope that they will enjoy birds
as much as I have

# Contents

# Contents

# Introduction

Altogether too many books have been written about watching birds. They have titles like 'Watching Birds', 'Bird-watching', 'Bird-watching and Bird Behaviour'. Few are actually about watching birds, most are simple introductions to avian biology with perhaps a general chapter thrown in for good measure covering binoculars and nest boxes. This book, I hope, is different. It treats bird-watching as a combination of skill and knowledge, as much an art as it is a science. Watching birds is an activity, a pastime, a hobby or an obsession. For many who catch the bug it can become paramount in their very existence. There is no known cure.

Though those who have been infected with the bug are unable to throw it off, they do not necessarily find it very easy to progress. There are many things that the beginner wants to know and to know quickly; but they are often hidden away, sometimes in books, but more often in the minds of those who watch. Understanding birds is only part of the skill – most bird-watchers ask the questions: What? Where? When? How? and just occasionally Why? I have attempted to answer four of these questions here. If your question is 'Why should I watch birds?' you should take up golf, sailing or knitting. Some bird-watchers do try to justify their activities in terms of studying birds to add to our knowledge, or to keep an eye on our environment. They should not bother to find excuses. I watch birds, I admit, because I can't stop doing it – and that is that as far as I am concerned.

To a bird-watcher the greatest compliment is to be told that he is 'good in the field'. It means that he can find and identify birds to a requisite, though unformulated, standard. It means that he has arrived. It is a standard that all beginners aim at and which those who persist usually achieve. But there are things that mark out some bird-watchers from the others – their ability to find birds where others have missed them, to identify birds that others find confusing, and to put a name to a bird with that certainty that only comes with long familiarity. I have been in the field with a great many good bird-watchers; some have stood out from the rest. Their qualities have been various, but their most important attribute has been honesty. The ability to say that they were wrong or uncertain. I have also met some bird-watchers who, lacking this quality, were in a class on their own. Such companions are best avoided.

Bird-watching is like plumbing – it is best learned on the job. Books can be helpful, they can encourage, inform and steer in the right direction, but they suffer from the disadvantage of being theoretical. This book is as practical as I can make it, but it is no substitute for outings with experienced bird-watchers in the field. Just as a course in the theory of plumbing does not enable a person to call himself a plumber, neither does reading a book produce a ready-made bird-watcher.

London, November 1974          JOHN GOODERS

# CHAPTER ONE

# How Birds Live

Birds are the most widespread and numerous of the larger animals and also the most obvious and easy to observe. In the 150 million years since they first appeared in the Jurassic period, they have occupied almost every part of the planet, apart from the polar regions. But even there, in the most hostile environment on earth, birds have penetrated within a few hundred miles of the two Poles.

Perhaps the most remarkable thing about the 8,600 species that inhabit the world today is their remarkable similarity one to another. No one, I would venture, would have any difficulty in identifying the vast majority of birds as birds. They may range from the large condors to the tiny wrens, but all are quite clearly birds. Just a very few may pose problems. The kiwi, for example, does not look very 'bird-like' and may be confused in the bizarre antipodean fauna that includes the duck-billed platypus and echidna. The ostrich, as well as the other large, flightless ratite species, are not typically 'birds'. But most birds are easy to identify as such.

## Flight

One of the most important factors in this apparent uniformity of appearance is the structural requirements necessary for flight. Almost all birds can fly, an aspect of their lives which makes them not only highly mobile and appealing, but also imposes strict limitations on their diversity. I does, for instance, limit their size. The heaviest flying birds weigh no more than forty pounds, whereas those that have successfully dispensed with the need to take to the air may weigh several hundreds of pounds. There is a complex inter-relationship between weight and power that effectively means that most birds, along with other flying animals, are small and light in weight.

The ostrich has dispensed with flight by developing long powerful legs and antelope-like feet. It avoids danger not by flying but by running very fast. Other species, notably rails, have dispensed with flight because of the lack of ground predators on their island homes. Once established on a predator-free island, these already weak fliers quickly adapted to new circumstances in geographical isolation. They had no need of flight. Only during the last century or so have these endemic rails suffered a decline due to human introductions of alien predators such as rats and cats. The flightless cormorant of the Galapagos Islands was able to dispense with flight simply because of the immense richness of the seas around its island home, whereas the world's other cormorants need to fly long distances to the richest fishing grounds.

The flightless cormorant still propels itself underwater with its huge webbed, paddle-like feet; whereas, those other marine fish eaters, the penguins and auks, have developed even further and swim beneath the surface with their wings. In the case of the penguins this process has been taken to the logical conclusion of flightlessness simply because of the safety of the areas they inhabit around the Antarctic continent and the southern seas. The northern auks, save the extinct great auk, never developed so far. They are thus not the perfect underwater fishermen that the penguins have become, nor are they very good fliers. Their wings serve two distinct functions, they are a compromise.

Birds are adapted to flight in a number of ways, and their ability to fly has a profound effect on their lives. But flight is, overall, the single most important factor in understanding birds.

## Feathers

Birds are covered with feathers that evolved from the scales of their reptilian ancestors. Feathers vary according to their function. The penguins, for example, have a waterproof covering of seal-like hairs that form a 'fur' to insulate them in the cold waters they inhabit. Their plumage is a marked contrast to that of the ostriches whose elaborate plumes serve different functions.

The feather is an acknowledged measurement of lightness: 'light as a feather' we say. Yet it is also the finest of insulators. We have down quilts as well as special arctic clothing made of eiderdown, and so far even the resources of a modern

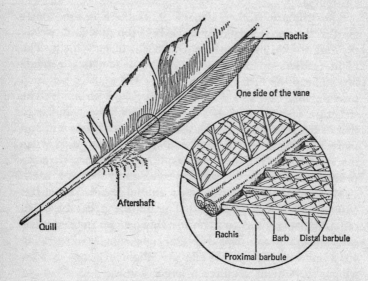

1. Structure of a flight feather shows the interlocking of barbs and barbules to form a solid air-resistant vane.

chemical industry have failed to produce a satisfactory substitute. Clearly if any animal had to evolve efficient insulation of the lightest possible material it would be one that flew. But birds have taken the need for weight saving to extremes in almost every aspect of their lives. The feathers of their wings that propel them through the air are both extremely light and extremely strong. The shaft of a primary feather is hollow, flexible, but very difficult to snap. It is bordered by an interlocking series of barbs that form an effective vane. When a bird's wing is pulled downwards the individual flight feathers overlap to form a continuous area. On the up-beat the feathers twist and open to allow air to pass freely between them. The fineness and lightness of a bird's primary feather never ceases to amaze children and it is a strange child that has not taken a found feather home. Many of us never get over collecting these remarkable structures.

The primary feathers (the long feathers on the outer joint of the wing) vary in number between nine and twelve, they are the major propellers, the means of movement. The flight feathers on the inner joint, the secondaries, provide lift, to keep the bird airborne. The feathers of the tail help provide lift, but also act as a rudder and airbrake. The structure of both secondaries and tail feathers is similar to that of the primaries, though they are generally less stiff and more pliable, to suit their function. Both groups are also more variable in number, between different species, than the primaries.

Modern aircraft fly at the most extraordinary speeds, but still have to slow down to land. The trouble is that these two requirements conflict to a considerable degree: the result has been the systems of flaps that alter the geometry of the wing on a modern airliner. While fast flight requires narrow wings, slow flight requires a larger surface area. Without larger wings the plane would either have to land unacceptably fast or it would stall. Birds have their own built-in anti-stall device in the form of a bastard wing. These four feathers grow from the bird's vestigial thumb and have the effect of smoothing out the flow of air over the wing and reducing stalling speed.

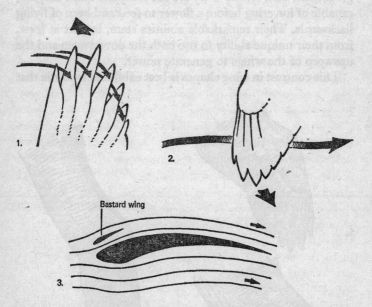

2. As a bird's wing is raised, the primary feathers open to allow air to pass between them. On the down stroke they overlap to form propulsive air-paddles. The bastard wing smooths the passage of air over the wing to prevent stalling.

While all flying birds have the basic wing and feather structure in common, the actual shape of the wing varies enormously. Some birds are highly aerial, fast fliers like the swifts. Their wings are long and pointed and their stream-lined body shape fits their mode of living. Vultures are also highly aerial, but they do not feed in the air and do not require the speed and agility of the swifts. Their long, broad wings enable them to circle slowly overhead, watchful for the signs of carrion, and their stalling speed is extremely low.

Hummingbirds have extremely long and attenuated wings that beat so fast that they produce the audible hum that gives them their name. They are the complete aerial masters, capable of hovering before a flower to feed and even of flying backwards. Their remarkable abilities stem, in part at least, from their unique ability to use both the downsweep and the upsweep of the wings to generate power.

This contrast in wing shapes is best exhibited by birds that

1.

2.

3.

3. The rounded wing of a grouse, the broad wing of a buzzard and the long narrow wing of an albatross all work in different ways suiting each species to a different mode of living.

live totally different types of life. Grouse, for example, are ground dwelling land birds that are resident and escape predation by concealment rather than flight. When forced into the air their rounded wings produce a sudden burst of acceleration and they then glide low over the ground before alighting. In sharp contrast the wings of the albatrosses are long, narrow gliding wings which support the bird with barely a flap. In this case propulsion is provided by the force of the wind in the oceanic wastes that they inhabit.

While the feathers of the wings and tail provide lift and propulsion in flight, these are not their only functions. In some groups, such as waders, they are boldly marked with bars that serve as identification and contact marks in fast-flying flocks. Some species, notably the pennant-winged nightjar, even have specially extended feathers that protrude from the wing and are part of territorial and nuptial displays. While such appendages are unusual and would clearly seem to impede a bird in flight, tail streamers are comparatively commonplace. The tail of the resplendent quetzal of South America is three times as long as the body; and nearer home the skuas have all evolved streamers in breeding plumage.

Body plumage does not only act as an insulator. Most birds are coloured, and for a variety of reasons. Many are camouflaged so as to avoid predators. Others are boldly coloured to attract mates or defend territories. Others have patches of bright colours that enable individuals of the same species to recognise one another. The family of bee-eaters, for example, look remarkably similar and are best identified by the areas of bright colour about the head. While we find such colour patches useful to name the various species there is no reason to suppose that the birds themselves do not utilise them for similar purposes.

## Structure

Though feathers may be the most obvious adaption to

flight, in fact the whole structure of birds is geared to providing the best power-weight ratios. Their bones are thin-walled and hollow and, where extreme strength is required, they are honeycombed. Muscle is reduced to a minimum. In fact the only really substantial areas of muscle on a bird are the flight muscles located on either side of the sternum or breast bone. These muscles, the breast of a chicken, are divided into two sets, the lower and larger

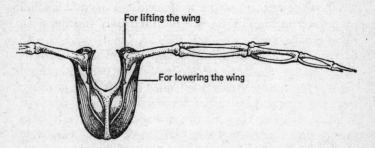

For lifting the wing

For lowering the wing

4. The bird's power house consists of the two sets of breast muscles that raise and lower the wing in flight.

which pulls the wing downwards on the propulsion stroke, and the upper which raises the wing ready for the next beat. This is the bird's 'engine-room', the necessary muscle to maintain powered flight which may account for half its total weight. In birds that glide, rather than beat their way through the air, these muscles may be reduced, while in some flightless birds they are virtually absent altogether.

All of a bird's other internal organs are reduced in size according to this weight reduction axiom. The digestive system, for example, is remarkably speedy and can deal with food, extracting the useful and discarding the waste, in a matter of minutes rather than hours. The female's ovaries form eggs extraordinarily quickly. A bird simply cannot afford the luxury of carrying around its young within its body for any length of time. The weight of a clutch of eggs would prove too much of a hindrance, impede its feeding ability and make it more likely to fall prey to predators. In fact, the system of laying eggs in a nest is ideal for flying animals that need to rear large numbers of young each year to maintain their numbers.

## Migration

The ability to fly makes birds the most highly mobile animals in the world. Some species like the Arctic tern fly from one end of the earth to the other every year; others make more modest journeys, while yet others seldom leave their tiny territories during their entire lives.

It is a fact of geography that large areas of the world are virtually uninhabitable for lengthy periods of the year. The land beyond the Arctic Circle is a hostile place in winter that supports only a few seed eaters, other vegetarians and the predators that prey on them. In summer, however, everything changes and the tundra becomes full of life while the sun shines twenty-four hours each day. Many creatures such as insects take advantage of this 'bloom' of life by hibernating or spending the winter in a state of suspended development.

Birds, however, with one notable exception* do not hibernate. Instead they migrate to these rich northern latitudes from the milder climes where they spend the winter. As a result huge numbers of birds, insectivorous passerines and aquatic waders, perform vast migrations. The numbers involved are staggering and the losses along the way stunning. But while individuals may die, the species as a whole must benefit. It is axiomatic that if a food source exists some species of bird will have evolved the ability to take advantage of it.

* The American poor-will, a nightjar, has been found hibernating in rocky crevices in California.

Migration has always fascinated man, but even as short a time ago as the eighteenth century the great migration-hibernation debate still raged. That we now know the answer does not mean that we know all about migration – far from it. We know that regular seasonal flights bring birds to our shores. We have a good idea where they winter. We know the routes some of them take and of seasonal variations in such routes. We know that most birds migrate below 4,000 feet, but that others cross the Himalayas at altitudes where man has been unable to penetrate without the aid of bottled oxygen. We know that many migrants are capable of covering long distances non-stop, flying from one day into the next. We know that they take on fuel in the form of fat prior to migrational flights and that some species may even double their 'normal' weight. We know that birds of prey and storks, because they are dependent on thermals of rising air generated by the heat of the sun on the land, avoid long sea crossings. And that many other birds migrate on a broad front and are not channelled along particularly favoured routes. These and many other aspects of bird migration we know about, but there are many unanswered questions and doubtless many questions that we have not even asked.

Even birds as large and obvious as the greater flamingo pose problems. There are, for example, 10,000 of these birds on the salt lakes of southern Cyprus every winter, but we do not know where they come from. Outside of Europe and North America, especially, the problems are immense.

## Life Cycles

British birds are comparatively well known, but there are still plenty of species in the world of which no ornithologist has ever seen a nest. A great many are forest birds inhabiting remote regions in the jungles of South America, but others are seabirds.

All birds lay eggs, but in their reproductive routines that

is about all they have in common. The malleefowl of Australia, for example, buries its eggs in a huge mound that acts as an artificial incubator. The adults simply regulate the temperature of the mound and when the chicks hatch they dig their way to the surface and are immediately independent. More typically, birds build a nest, lay a clutch of several eggs, incubate them and feed the resulting chicks until they fledge and are ready for a life of their own. Such routines are common among birds throughout the world, though the time taken, number of eggs, incubation period, nest structure and nest site, fledging period and the roles of the sexes varies enormously.

Some species like the blue tit turn over very quickly. They lay large clutches, rear many young, but still only maintain their population from one year to the next. The wastage rate is very high indeed and the average fledged blue tit can expect to live only a few months. The fulmar, however, lays only a single egg and even then only begins to breed when it is seven years old. It has little to fear from predators out on the open ocean and the only possible limitations on its population are the supply of food and nest sites. Certainly the average fulmar can expect to live for several years.

## Behaviour

Birds are comparatively simple animals and much of their behaviour can be interpreted by a simple stimulus–response theory. Human behaviour is more complex and the behaviourist theory of psychology does us less than justice when it moves from the interpretation of animal behaviour to the interpretation of human acts. Birds respond to stimuli with responses that have evolved along with their structure. In both they are fitted to their environment. When they are confused, or when confronted with a stimulus to which they have no established response, they often perform 'silly' or irrelevant acts that we generally refer to as displacement activities. These may take a variety of forms, but preening is one of the more commonplace responses produced by confusion.

Many cock birds establish a breeding territory which they defend against other males of the same species. They protect their little patch by song, by posture and by fighting. The territory may also be a feeding ground of sufficient size to sustain the bird, its mate and their offspring. In general it could be argued that the number of birds, that is the total population, is determined by the amount of food available. But some ornithologists have argued that it is social factors – that is the number of territories and therefore breeding units that an area can accommodate – that determines the population level. Whatever the answer it is clear that territory is crucial to the successful breeding of birds.

In the case of the familiar blackbird, a territory may be less than an acre, while a golden eagle may consider several thousand acres as his domain. But a gannet colony consists of nests evenly spaced about a yard apart covering the top of some flat-topped holm, and the individual's territory extends only as far as it can reach with its sharp bill.

Yet other species have only tiny territories within an established display ground. Blackcock, for example, gather at a lek, as it is called, every morning and evening to display one to another to ensure that their own little patch is not invaded by their neighbours. When a female, called a greyhen, appears on the scene she selects one of the males to mate with. The advantage to the species is that within his tiny territory each male is king and his love-making will not be disturbed.

The male blackbird maintains his territory throughout the year, though less rigorously through the winter. In spring he sings loud and long to proclaim his ownership of a certain, to him at least, well-defined piece of countryside. The essential ingredients within this territory are the existence of a nest site or two, several song posts and opportunities to feed. His neighbour will have a similar territory roughly the same size and incorporating the same facilities. If one male dies his place will be taken within days, sometimes within hours, by another male previously without a place to call his own. The adoption of a territorial system such as this has the immense advantage of spreading blackbirds evenly throughout suitable habitat. Should such a system break down, as it

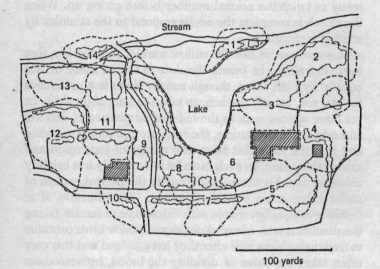

5. Fourteen territories of robins in a suburban area of large gardens. Note that fences, roads and even islands have little effect on the nature of the territories, but that there is little vacant ground.

did following the severe winter of 1962–3, then birds will be confused and spend much of their time disputing the boundaries of their territories instead of getting on with the important duties of rearing a family. What happened in 1963 was that a majority of established blackbirds had been killed during the winter and that new birds moving in lacked the composite knowledge that their predecessors had established of territorial boundaries.

Though birds cannot apparently count, or at least not very well, they do have some sense of quantity. If one egg is found in a nest and every subsequent egg is removed as it is laid the hen will continue to lay to try to produce her normal clutch of five or six. Some birds have been induced to lay as many as twice the normal number before giving up. When the clutch is complete the adults respond to the stimulus by starting incubation.

In some species like the willow warbler it is the hen that incubates alone. In others the duty is shared more or less equally by both sexes, though usually there is a preference for one sex, usually the hen, to take the long night shift. In yet other species such as the red-necked phalarope, dotterel and other migrant waders, the roles are completely reversed and it is the male that takes sole charge of incubation and care of the young. In such cases he is invariably less brightly coloured than his mate, in contrast to the normal pattern of males being more brightly coloured. The situation after hatching is equally variable with either male or female taking the dominant role. Many of our more familiar birds continue to feed their chicks well after they have fledged and this very often takes the form of dividing the brood, between them though in some cases the male takes charge of the entire brood enabling the female to get on with the business of constructing a new nest for a second brood.

## Voice

Birds are very vocal animals. They sing in proclamation of their ownership of a territory, but also exhibit a whole range of other calls which fulfil a variety of functions. The alarm calls, the '*tak-tak*' of the robin and the chuckling scolding of a blackbird are familiar sounds of a British woodland. They serve to alert other creatures, as well as others of their kind, to the approach of danger.

Birds spend much of their time in groups outside the breeding season and maintain the composition of the flock with contact notes. But though a large variety of different calls have been described for different species, it is song that appeals most to our ears and which is such a part of the countryside in spring.

Most birds have a simple song like the oft-repeated three notes of the song thrush, or the delicate '*chiff-chaff-chiff-chaff*' of the chiffchaff. But others, like many of the warblers, have a fine array of notes that seems almost to have an ascetic quality. The nightingale is renowned in this respect, but the blackcap is no mean performer either. Woodpeckers are instrumentalists beating out their territorial claims on suitably chosen dead branches which produce a 'drumming' that echoes through the woods and forests. Snipe produce a strange 'song' by diving in the sky so that the air passing through their stiff outer tail feathers produces a beating sound as they circle their marshy territories.

The nightingale, its fine virtuosity apart, is also unusual in producing a strange duet between male and female consisting of a low whistle followed by a croak from the female. Many tropical birds have developed such dueting habits into quite elaborate 'part singing'. The colourful boubou shrikes of the African savannahs are particularly good examples, in which it is very difficult to tell whether one or two birds are involved and which is which. These birds are also unusual in being both brightly coloured and highly vocal. Usually it is the small, more dully coloured birds that have the loudest and most distinctive songs. The nightingale, a dull, undistinguished brown bird, is a case in point and so too is the wren. If a bird is large, colourful and obvious it has little need of a song to attract a mate. The displaying male ostrich, for example, is a remarkable sight. Crouched on its haunches it opens its black and white wings and flashes them alternately with a peculiar rolling motion, all the while slapping its gyrating neck against its body with a loud smack. With such a large bird and such an obvious display, song is irrelevant.

## Bills, Feet and Food

Birds can be divided into a large number of categories on the basis of their food. Indeed they are adapted to take a wide variety of foods. Some are remarkably conservative in their feeding habits like the crossbill which has a bill specially adapted to opening tough pine cones and extracting the seeds. Presented with a bird, an ornithologist can tell a lot about its life simply by studying its bill and its feet. It may, for instance, have a thin insect-eating bill, or a wide gape indicating that it catches its insect food in the air. It may have the long probing bill of a wader such as a godwit or curlew, or the thick chunky bill of a hawfinch suited to cracking hard nuts. Eagles have sharply hooked bills suitable for tearing flesh, though prey is invariably taken with the sharp clasping talons. Ospreys have specially serrated talons suitable for grasping slippery fish which they hunt by diving into the water from the air. Another fish-eater the red-breasted merganser has a serrated bill for similar reasons. Woodpeckers have chisel-like bills, spoonbills have sifting bills, herons' bills are dagger-like and hummingbirds' fine pipe-like tubes. Each is adapted to a particular food source. But other birds are all-rounders capable of taking any opportunity that presents itself. Starlings are particularly good examples of all-rounders, a fact which helps to explain their extraordinary world-wide success.

Just as their bills vary according to food, so do birds' feet vary according to their habitats. Duck have webbed feet and grebes semi-palmated ones. Waders have long legs, and the almost totally aerial swifts and swallows very short ones. Jacanas, often called lilytrotters, have long toes to spread their weight over floating aquatic vegetation, while the foot of the ostrich has been reduced to two toes suitable for running. The 'normal' foot of the average perching bird consists of three toes pointing forwards and one backwards.

6. As the major means of feeding, bills can tell us a great deal about the way of life of a bird. The eagle is a flesh-tearer; the curlew a mud-prober; the crossbill a seed-extracter; and the hawfinch a nut-cracker.

It is a simple grasping mechanism and is seldom used for anything but perching, though keen bird-gardeners will know that blue tits and others sometimes grasp food in their feet like a raptor.

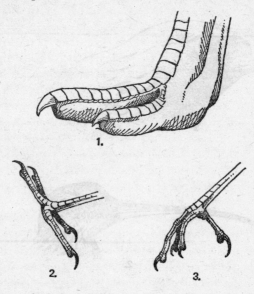

7. Feet are adapted to different modes of living – the running 'hoof' of the ostrich; the clinging foot of the woodpecker; the grasping foot of a perching bird.

## Listing the Birds

Beginners are often puzzled by the way in which birds appear in bird books. Why, they ask, are the birds not arranged alphabetically? There is no simple answer to this, save that the usual method of arranging the birds, the systematic approach, does have the distinct advantage of placing similar birds next to one another. This may be confusing at first, but has distinct advantages once you have learned to find your way about the order.

The next question follows a little later: why do some books put birds in one order and another put them completely differently? The full answer to this is also complex, though it is simple enough to say that there is nothing to stop any author putting birds into any order he likes providing he can find someone to publish the result.

The trouble really stems from the fact that there is no universally agreed order for listing birds. There are a few guide-lines, like placing the most primitive species first and the most advanced last, though some writers have turned this around and started with the most advanced. Moreover not only do we not agree about the start and the end, but there is continuing debate about the place of many bird families within the list. Ultimately it boils down to the fact that we ask conflicting things from our lists of birds. We require them to fulfil different functions which they are incapable of doing simultaneously.

The bird-watcher wants a list of birds in English which is stable, in line with modern usage and which will enable him to isolate one bird from another and put a name to it. The ornithologist wants much the same, save that he needs scientific (Latin) names as well, so that relationships are more easily made clear. The systematist, the man ultimately responsible for naming and arranging the birds, wants none of these things. It is part and parcel of his trade to investigate the very relationships which systematic lists seek to present and, if he is successful in his work, he will wish to change the name of a species and move its position within the list. Ultimately the systematist is heading towards a state of perfection in which every bird is correctly placed and named and the subtleties of the evolutionary process are reflected in a single list of birds. Such a Utopia seems a long way off.

The systematic naming of birds is based on the scheme proposed by Carl von Linné (the name is usually Latinised to Linneaus) in which every form of life is classified into different Classes. Thus all birds are placed in the class *Aves*.

Within each class animals are divided into orders, within each order into different families, within each family into different genera, and, finally, within each genus into different species. The species is the ultimate unit of zoology. Various sub-groupings such as sub-family, super-species and sub-species are also used, but are of little concern to the bird-watcher. An example may help to make the system more clear. Consider the nightingale:

> Class    = *Aves*
> Order    = *Passeriformes*
> Family   = *Muscicapidae*
> Genus    = *Luscinia*
> Species = *Luscinia megarhynchos*

Thus the nightingale bears the scientific name of *Luscinia megarhynchos* which, by established tradition, is always printed in italics. It is a member of the genus *Luscinia* which also includes closely related birds such as the bluethroat *Luscinia svecica*. Where members of the same genus are scientifically named one after another the abbreviation *L.* replaces the full *Luscinia*. Thus the Siberian rubythroat would be listed as *L. calliope*.

While Latin names are precise they are not, as we have seen, fixed. Indeed they cannot be fixed simply because of the nature of the systematist's work. One writer has likened the pursuit of systematic perfection to looking down on the canopy of a tree where all the leaves can be seen, but where the branches and twigs that bear them remain hidden from sight. In his work the systematist is trying by every possible means to ascertain the evolutionary relationships between birds, to see which evolved when, and how they fit together. To ask him to stabilise a list of Latin names for our convenience is to ask the impossible.

Strange as it may seem there is a perfectly good method of stabilising bird names based on the vernacular English names. Yet ornithologists show an extraordinarily arrogant disregard, almost contempt, for vernacular names, and bird-watchers seem unable to get together to produce a list for their own use. Even a vernacular list would not be absolutely stable. As views on the position of a particular bird changed so would its position within the list. Thus the robin might be moved from the genus *Erithacus* to join the nightingale and bluethroat in the genus *Luscinia*, and instead of being *Erithacus rubecula* it would become *Luscinia rubecula*. But its English name would remain the same, which I happen to think would be a considerable advantage.

All species are named with what we call a Latin binomial (generic and specific names). Sub-species receive a Latin trinomial. The British robin, for example, is *Erithacus rubecula melophilus* – it has a Latin trinomial. At one time all bird books were full of trinomials with hosts of birds being referred to as the British this, and the British that, as if there was a considerable difference between a British bird and its continental counterpart. With a few minor exceptions, such as the pied and white wagtails and the continental and British lesser black-backed gulls, it is impossible to pick out a sub-species in the field. It is, therefore, of little concern to the bird-watcher.

This book is about bird-watching, not about birds. I happen to believe that many people get a great deal of enjoyment out of their hobby, pastime and passion. I also believe that the more the bird-watcher understands of the life of his quarry the more enjoyment he will receive. This chapter has just scratched the surface of the life of birds. No book can say all we know about birds, though many have tried. There is much to be said for finding out for yourself.

CHAPTER TWO

# How to Watch Birds

Bird-watching is one of the boom departments of the twentieth-century leisure industry. Like sailing, water-skiing, fishing, golf, squash, mountain climbing and canoeing it has experienced an incredible upsurge of interest and activity. But while a golfer plays golf and a sailor sails, what does a bird-watcher do? He could be studying the courtship behaviour of the greenfinch, or attempting a big day list. He could be on a country ramble, or watching the birds in his garden. He may be ringing or censusing. In fact a whole range of activities qualify as 'bird-watching' and, as a result, bird-watchers get pleasure and satisfaction from their hobby in a variety of different ways.

Unlike most other hobbies, watching birds has tradi-tionally suffered from scientific overtones. It has been considered a part of science, rather than a sport or pastime. As a result books about bird-watching have been usually introductions to ornithology. The beginner at birds feels rather guilty if he does not join in some form of co-operative research or start an intensive study of his own. Gradually he may outgrow this feeling, but he will never completely escape it. Some, then, may wish to be amateur ornithologists while others are happy simply seeing birds – both, I venture, will get more from their hobby by knowing more about their quarry. Without a framework of knowledge our watching lacks structure. A new bird must be identified, but putting a name to a bird is in itself only a part of our language game. If someone saw an ostrich but did not know what it was called, he would still be able to say 'I have seen a new bird – a lifer'. Doubtless he would recognise it again for such a distinguished bird is hard to forget. But if instead of an ostrich he saw a species of sunbird, he would be unlikely to recognise it again unless he had been able to put a name to it to pick it out from other sunbirds. Without labels of this sort most birds would be unidentifiable, but putting a label on a bird is only the beginning.

The pleasure of seeing a new bird is in proportion to the amount of knowledge that we have of the species concerned. Fly an ocean and you will see a 'lifer', but so what? How can this compare with the pleasure obtained from seeing a new bird at home, or finding a species that has been missed for years?

The pleasure obtained from watching birds is dependent on our knowledge of their lives and on the skill with which we pursue them. This book is about knowledge and skill and the pleasure that we get from their exercise, and not about making judgements concerning what bird-watchers should or should not do. Watching birds is, after all, a pleasure.

## Field Guides

Watching birds needs little in the way of equipment, indeed you can watch and enjoy them without anything at all. But most of us find it essential to identify what we see and the first tool of any bird-watcher is his field guide. Strange as it may seem field guides are a comparatively recent invention dating only from the 1930s. The first was Roger Tory Peterson's *A Field Guide to the Birds* covering all of the species that occur in eastern North America. Only in 1954 did a similar guide appear to cover the birds of Britain and Europe. Basically field guides illustrate every species known to occur in a geographical area and the text is designed to complement the picture by picking out features that cannot be shown visually, such as how it moves and flies, where it lives, whether or not it migrates and so on.

Ideally every species should be illustrated in colour, arranged so as to facilitate comparison and in a characteristic pose. The text and a distribution map should be immediately next to the illustration so that the full details of a bird are all on the same page spread. Unfortunately the economics of printing and publishing are such that an ideal arrangement like this inevitably leads to a very reduced area being available for text. With many species text is almost irrelevant anyway, but with the very species that are difficult to identify the cutting down on text is sufficient to make the book fail in its purpose.

Four current field guides are available to the European bird-watcher:

*A Field Guide to the Birds of Britain and Europe* by Roger Tory Peterson, Guy Mountfort and P. A. D. Hollom, Collins, London.
First published in 1954 this immediately became the bird-watchers' field guide and has been in general use ever since. It has been revised twice with the addition of new plates at the end, but at the time of writing is beginning to look rather dated. Its strong points are the quite excellent paintings by Roger Peterson and the room available for text and maps, both of which are good. Its drawback – that information on a single bird (and similar and confusing species) is scattered and often separated by many pages. Nevertheless it is *the* book at the moment simply because it is so accurate.

*The Pocket Guide to British Birds* by R. S. R. Fitter and Richard Richardson, Collins, London.
Though it appeared earlier than the Peterson guide and was apparently replaced by it, this book continues to sell well and is still in print more than twenty years after being published. The paintings are very good, but the book

suffers from being arranged under the totally false and misleading arrangement of habitats. Birds are far too mobile to be confined to either a breeding or wintering habitat. They may prefer marshes, but will end up in all manner of other unlikely spots during the course of the year. Such an arrangement also leads to similar and closely related birds being scattered, rather than grouped together for comparison.

*The Hamlyn Guide to Birds of Britain and Europe* by Bertel Brunn and Arthur Singer, Hamlyn, London.
The first of the soft back guides, the first in full colour throughout and the first to utilise the logical unit of a two-page spread as a base unit. Though Arthur Singer is a great bird artist, his work is not as clinical as that needed for a field guide. What's more, being an American, he lacks the familiarity with European birds, especially the more obscure species, that is so necessary for such a work. The text is short and often not enlightening. The two-colour maps are a good innovation, but are often inaccurate.

*The Birds of Britain and Europe* by Hermann Heinzel, Richard Fitter and John Parslow, Collins, London.
The ultimate soft-back, covering an extra area that makes it virtually a field guide to the western Palearctic region. It enjoys and suffers from the two-page spread format. The paintings are very good, though some species reveal an unfamiliarity on the artist's part and the text is limited by space. The latter is sometimes irrelevant to field identification and on occasion virtually useless. But covering a larger number of species the book is extremely handy and the maps are the best ever produced.

The majority of bird-watchers take their Peterson and their Heinzel-Fitter with them wherever they travel. No doubt the ultimate field guide will eventually appear, with the merits of both within a single volume.

The Collins-Peterson Field Guide series is progressively covering more and more parts of the world. For the travelling bird-watcher their acquisition is the first step in planning a journey. Few are as good as the European books (save those that cover North America), but their scope and coverage is limited by the lower potential sales in less bird-conscious areas of the world.

## Handbooks

Most bird-watchers are book collectors. They obtain almost as much pleasure from reading about birds as they do from seeing them. Even if reading is regarded as a simple means-end relationship to improve their chances of enjoyable field outings, they still need a formidable library. First and foremost are the books, often called 'Handbooks', that detail the lives of their local birds. Handbooks are available covering most areas of the world, though they vary in quality and price, and some important works are out of print and very expensive. Covering Britain and Europe we have:

*The Handbook of British Birds* by H. F. Witherby *et al*, Witherby, London. The standard book in five volumes on British birds, including a host of rarities that have occurred on only a few occasions. If something is not in 'The Handbook', as it is affectionately known, then it is probably new knowledge. It is the Bible of British ornithology, though being nearly forty years old it is in need of revision. It will be replaced by:

*The Birds of the Western Palearctic* by Stanley Cramp *et al* which has been due to appear for several years and is planned as a multi-volume work covering every species found in this vast area. No doubt, when it appears and is completed, it will be a fine and expensive book, and one that will be indispensable to every serious ornithologist and a great many bird-watchers.

*Handbuch der Vögel Mitteleuropas* by U.N. Glutz von Blotzheim, Akademische Verlagsgesellschaft, Frankfurt. This is a tremendous multi-volume book in process of publication. It devotes up to twenty or more large pages to each bird and is the most detailed account of the species included ever published. Every aspect of what we know about the birds is detailed. Unfortunately, though it covers most of the birds that occur in Britain, its strangely old-fashioned geographical limits preclude an English translation. A great pity, for this is the ultimate handbook.

*The Birds of the British Isles* by D. A. Bannerman, Oliver and Boyd, Edinburgh.
One of those curious nineteenth-century type works produced by Dr Bannerman in the middle of this century. Though it covers all the British birds in twelve volumes, his discursive and flowing style makes it difficult to get at the facts, while being laced with taxonomics of his own. It is a good read and there is much interesting material tucked away between its covers.

*The Popular Handbook of British Birds* by P. A. D. Hollom, Witherby, London.
An abridged version of 'The Handbook' in one volume. All the basic facts of British birds can be found under neat headings and several revisions have added considerably to its value. It is a fine book for the beginner.

## Other Books

Books on more specialised aspects of birds are legion and it would be a strange bird-watcher who had not read:

*The Life of the Robin* by David Lack, Penguin, Middlesex. A fine monograph that both reads well and gets to the very heart of the life of this most interesting bird. In particular it deals with territory in a very clear and concise way.

*The Yellow Wagtail* by Stuart Smith, Collins, London.
This is another excellent monograph, one of the best of
the New Naturalist series of accounts of a single species.
Another is:

*The Fulmar* by James Fisher, Collins, London.
The encyclopaedic mind of the late James Fisher was
ideally adapted to delving into every source for information and *The Fulmar* remains a tribute to a fine and very
influential ornithologist.

Bird-watchers are progressively ridding themselves of
national and continental shackles and becoming more
conscious of the whole world of birds. Several books have
covered this in their various ways, though a single usable
check-list of all the birds has not yet appeared.*

*Birds of the World* by Oliver L. Austin Jnr. and Arthur
Singer, Hamlyn, London.
A splendid book covering all of the bird families one by
one. It is easy to read and packed with information.

*The World of Birds* by James Fisher and Roger Tory
Peterson, MacDonald, London.
This book has a different approach. It covers all the bird
families together with maps of their distribution, but also
deals with ornithology and bird-watching on a world-wide
basis. It has a multi-faceted approach and is a storehouse
of information.

*Birds of the World* edited by John Gooders, IPC, London.
Originally published in parts to make ten volumes; it deals
in detail with over a quarter of the world's birds, but is
now out of print. Of course I am biased, but I hear it is a
useful book.

* Pre-publication announcements indicate that this situation will
soon be remedied.

*Birds – a Survey of the Bird Families of the World* by John Gooders, Hamlyn, London.
Another account of the world's birds family by family, in a single volume and illustrated with photographs. It suffers from a bias towards living birds in the field that reflects my own interests.

Bird-watching adventure stories properly belong to a former age and the works of Abel Chapman, Seebohm, Lodge and others have become minor classics – out of print and often expensive. More recent accounts of bird-watchers actually watching birds are:

*Portrait of a Wilderness* by Guy Mountfort, David & Charles, Devon. One knowledgeable critic likened this to the Field Guide in narrative form. *Portrait of a River* was a less appealing successor and *The Vanishing Jungle* (Collins, London) a fine account of expeditions to Pakistan and Bangladesh in search of birds, mammals and conservation opportunities.

*Wild America* by Roger Tory Peterson and James Fisher. A splendid account of the birds seen by these two colleagues during a lengthy trip around North America. Its appeal to the European watcher is that Fisher provides us with an account of his own reactions to a new fauna.

In regard to general bird-watching there are a host of books available. My own career started with:

*Watching Birds* by James Fisher, Penguin, Middlesex.
A book that acts as a basic introduction to ornithology while accommodating the enthusiasms of the author. For years I suffered under the delusion that all bird-watchers kept three separate card indexes covering all the birds of the world as advocated by Fisher. I'm glad to say that they don't.

*Collins Guide to Bird-watching* by R. S. R. Fitter, Collins, London.

This is a good guide and introduction with sections on all British birds and a list of where to find them.

*Nomina Avium Europaearum* by Harriet I. Jørgensen, Munksgaard, Copenhagen.

An invaluable little book that gives the names of all European birds in all European languages. Published in Denmark, it is difficult to obtain.

My own contribution to this section:

*Where to Watch Birds* and *Where to Watch Birds in Europe* by John Gooders, Deutsch, London.*

These are guides to the best bird-watching spots in Britain and Europe respectively. My aim to get people to the exact spot to see and enjoy birds. Both were brought up to date and revised in 1974.

## Sounds

If identifying the birds on sight is the most important basic skill required of the bird-watcher, the recognition of their calls runs it a close second. Personally I have always found bird songs and calls very difficult to remember – perhaps I have a visual memory rather than an audio one. Nevertheless being able to put a name to the single note issuing from a bush or forest, marsh or hill, has obvious advantages. Some very good bird-watchers that I know are short-sighted, but their ear for a call more than compensates for this inadequacy. Walk through a woodland with a real expert and the odd squeaks and chirrups quickly become species. The resultant saving in labour is enormous, for time spend stalking a strange sound that turns out to be a common bird is time wasted.

Most of our birds have distinctive songs and many are easy to learn. The repeated whistle of the song thrush, the flute-like calls and odd grunts of the nightingale, the fine warbling

* *Where to Watch Birds* is published in paperback by Pan Books.

of the blackcap – these are easy. The grating churrs of sedge and reed warblers need more practice; while to pick out the difference in pitch of the grasshopper and Savi's warblers needs a trained ear.

Undoubtedly the best way of learning song is to go out on regular field trips with an expert and not to be afraid to ask what sounds are what. Bird-watchers are notoriously proud people and feel that they ought to know what bird is responsible for every squeak that issues from a hedgerow. As a result they miss opportunities to learn from their companions. Perhaps if you ask next time an unidentified chirrup comes your way, you will find out that your companions do not know either.

Much can be learned from gramophone records or cassettes that are now available covering a great many birds from many parts of the world.

'Witherby's Sound Guide to British Birds' by Myles North and Eric Simms is really very good and covers the songs of a great many British breeding birds. It comes on a series of twelve-inch long playing records.

'A South-guide to the Birds of Europe' by Jean-Claude Roché, Institut Echo, France (available from Discourses Ltd, Tunbridge Wells, Kent) is an ambitious attempt to produce recordings of all European birds in a series of volumes. These volumes are geographically based, i.e., Western Europe, Northern Europe and so on, and there is thus an area of overlap of species. But Western Europe covers 256 different species and nearly 400 species are covered altogether.

'BBC Wildlife Series', BBC Radio Enterprises, London, is a series of records by well-known recordists such as Eric Simms and Ludwig Koch covering distinct regions of Britain. They are generally full of birds.

'Listen, The Birds', RSPB, Sandy, Bedfordshire, is a

series of six records crammed with solos by the most common of British songsters. It is a fine introduction to bird song and invaluable to anyone wanting to 'mug-up' his calls.

## Optics

Observation of birds, as well as other wildlife and sporting occasions, is made so much easier with binoculars that it is always a wonder that so many authors say that you can start watching birds without them. Of course you can, but it will be a very superficial or frustrating experience. Bird-watchers need binos, shifties, glasses or whatever else you call them.

Binoculars fall into three basic types: straight-through magnifiers, prismatic glasses, and the new roof-prism type.

Straight-through magnifying binoculars simply take the image and magnify it in the manner of an ordinary pair of opera glasses. They are of limited performance and value and suffer from a narrow field of view. They are better than nothing – just.

Prismatic binoculars are used by the vast majority of bird-watchers. They are a standard tool, but one which needs much care in the choosing. Binoculars can be obtained for all sorts of purposes. Sailors need a robust water-proof pair; flying enthusiasts a very powerful pair with which they can read numbers over long distances; coastguards have similar requirements but can afford to be less mobile and thus choose a heavy pair to be mounted on a tripod. Bird-watchers have conflicting needs and have, of necessity, to compromise.

The most important factors in choosing the right binoculars are size and weight, magnification, twilight value and field of view. But first a decision must be made between those instruments that have independent eye-piece focusing and those in which a control wheel focuses both eye-pieces together, with one eye-piece adjustable to compensate for individual discrepancies between the eyes. For all but very specialised uses, the central focusing type are to be preferred.

Size and weight are important. Binoculars may be slung around the neck for hour after hour and a heavy pair can become very tiring. What's more they are tiring to hold in use and more difficult to keep steady on a moving target. The major factor in weight is the size of the object lens – that is the one at the front of the binocular. A heavy pair with an object lens of 50 mm diameter is generally too heavy for all but the largest people, while a pair with a 60 mm object lens is altogether too heavy and bulky for birdwatching. If you visit a well-equipped bird reserve you will find that some hides are equipped with huge binoculars firmly mounted on tripods. They are excellent to use, but try carrying them around your neck on a strap!

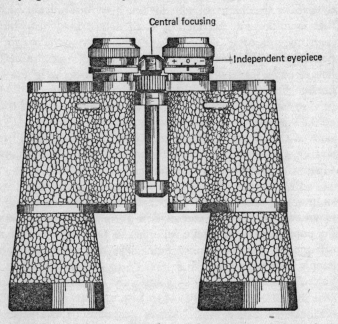

8. Prismatic binoculars with central focusing and independent eyepiece to allow for discrepancies between the eyes.

Magnification is important, if it was not you would not use binoculars at all. But the higher the magnification the smaller the field of view and the less light is passed through to the eye. With really high magnifications the subject tends to dance about before your eyes, you just cannot hold them still. Thus 'Super-de-luxe Cross Channel' binoculars are useless for bird-watching. They must be used on a tripod or by some other means of support. An ideal magnification for our purposes is ×7, ×8, ×9 or ×10. Again it's a matter of how strong you are. Ladies would be well advised to use the lower magnifications, gentlemen the higher. I use ×10, but there is no point in going higher than that.

Field of view is the size of the picture you see through the eye-piece. It is significant because the wider the field of view the greater the chance of your picking up a bird quickly; and that is important, particularly with a bird in flight. But high magnifications cut down the field of view. To compensate and produce a larger field of view a larger object lens must be incorporated, and that means more weight and greater size. Thus the field of view of an average pair of 7 × 30 binoculars (where the 7 is the magnification and the 30 the diameter of the object lens in millimetres) is about the same as that of a pair of 9 × 50. The difference in weight is startling. Incidentally, field of view is expressed in so many yards across at 1,000 yards' distance.

Twilight value, stressed by so many manufacturers, is simply the diameter of the object lens divided by the magnification. Thus a pair of $8 × 30 = 30 ÷ 8 = 3·7$. As the pupil of the human eye will open to 5 mm or 6 mm, it is capable of absorbing more light than the binoculars can supply. Thus a pair of $8 × 40 = 40 ÷ 8 = 5$ is much better. Of course this is of value only in poor light or in twilight when your pupil is open to the fullest in its search for light. So-called 'night glasses' are simply those with a higher twilight factor than the human eye is wide. They absorb more light than the eye can cope with.

So choice centres around magnification, weight and field of view. You will find that 7 × 30 is good, 8 × 30 first class, 9 × 35 first class, 10 × 50 first class and 12 × 50 virtually impossible. Choose a pair within these specifications to suit yourself and your pocket.

Clearly a pair of glasses that costs £10 will not give the same results as a pair that costs £100. The differences are complex, but basically centre around the care and work that goes into polishing the lenses, the number of lenses used, and the craftsmanship and accuracy with which the glasses are assembled. A cheap pair may be perfectly usable but may strain your eyes, be thrown out of alignment at the merest knock and have a narrow field of view. The better manufacturers create a wider field of view than the cheaper ones, but more important they give a precision instrument through which years and years of bird-watching can be enjoyed. Actually they are cheap at the price.

When purchasing a pair of binoculars spend what you can afford. Currently most instruments on sale below £20 are rubbish. Stick to names that you know like Leitz, Swift, Ross and Carl Zeiss, or the newer but well-established Japanese companies such as Nikon and Yashica.

I have always thought that second-hand binoculars are a particularly good buy. But they are precision instruments and there is a risk, albeit a small one, that an expensive repair bill may await a new owner. It is difficult to judge, but then how many people bother with a report on a used car when they spend ten times the amount of money that they will spend on a pair of binoculars?

## New roof-prism binoculars

The new type of prismatic binocular, made by Leitz and West German Carl Zeiss and brand-named Trinovid and Dialyt respectively, look like a straight through glass. They contain, however, an elaborate system of prisms, just like traditional binoculars save only that they are reduced to a more compact arrangement. Performance-wise they are quite excellent, but they also have the great advantage of having no external moving parts and are thus completely dust-proof. It is well known that I use a pair of West German Zeiss 10 × 40B Dialyt. They are expensive, but they are superb.

## Binoculars in Use

Binoculars will give better service if they are used properly and cared for at all times. With a new pair you must first adjust them to your eyes. One eye-piece will be marked with the numbers −3 2 1 0 1 2 3+. Shut that eye and look through the binoculars with the other eye open. Focus the central wheel or bar until a prominent object is perfectly focused. Then open the other eye and without touching the central wheel turn the eye-piece until both eyes are clearly in focus. Note the exact position of the number on the independent eye-piece and ensure that on all future occasions the number is in the same place.

'Break' the binoculars so that when you look through them you see a single circle. If you cannot achieve a single circle or experience a strain, send them at once to a qualified optical engineer. The eyes can learn to accommodate minor mis-alignments and will even attempt to compensate for large discrepancies. It is not worth letting them try to do so.

If you drop your binoculars (you will), check them thoroughly for chips and cracks, but on no account open them up. If you drop them in water (you will eventually) send them off straight away: to wait is to court disaster. While some repairs can be put off, water continues its work inside and may well cost you the price of a new pair. If you get an expensive pair get them insured along with your cameras and telescope.

Caring for your optics makes sense. A regular cleaning will

improve clarity and the amount of light that will pass through to your eyes. But only clean the exterior surfaces. A soft camera brush removes dust and grit and the optics can then be cleaned with a soft cloth or a chamois. Despite popular belief breathing on lenses does not usually damage them.

Sometimes controls become stiff and on occasion seize up altogether. Do not set to with the oil can, but have them seen to by a professional.

Many makers produce a plastic eye-piece cover that simply slips up and down on the neck strap and covers the eye-pieces when required. Such an aid is invaluable in a country where rain is an occupational hazard, but it is also a useful protection against dust.

## Telescopes

There are three basic types of telescope suitable for bird-watching. All are awkward in use, but they have the advantage of higher magnification than binoculars and are ideal for use on marshes and reservoirs when attempting to identify birds at great distances. They are also useful if confronted with a small bird at close range when diagnostic features such as wing bars and comparative length of primaries and secondaries may be beyond the scope of binoculars.

At one time I used a lightweight telescope on a tripod in preference to binoculars, but I am sure now that that was a mistake.

Traditional telescopes are made of brass with three or four pulls and fixed magnification of × 25 or × 30. Some have interchangeable eye-pieces. A well-known ornithologist once likened these instruments to looking through something about the same size and weight as a cormorant. They are unmanageable and are inferior to modern designs.

The modern telescope is a lightweight instrument con-structed of alloy with only two pulls. The object lens is usually 60 mm and magnification variable at the turn of the eye-piece from × 15 or × 20 to × 60. Focusing is via a positive knurled knob, rather than by pushing the final pull in and out as with the traditional telescope. They still need to be supported, either by a knee when lying down, or by a post, tree or tripod. There is little to choose between the Nickel Supra or the Hertel and Reuss. Both are similar in design, performance and price. They are light and compact to carry and come in a handy case with shoulder strap.

The idea of a prismatic telescope is an obvious one, but manufacturers have been slow to realise their potential and only one British manufacturer has produced one. Several makes, however, are available in the United States and one in Sweden. I have used the latter on several occasions and found it quite the equal of the Nickel Supra lightweight, save only that to change magnification the eye-piece has to be removed and replaced with another. It is thus impossible to find the bird on low power before zooming in to a higher magnification. Optically, however, it is first rate and it is a great pity that no distributor has the enterprise to import it into the UK.

## Notebooks

All bird-watchers keep notebooks if only to congratulate themselves on seeing a good bird or on having a good day. For many it enables them to refer back to a particular day or a particular place and no more; while others are methodical in writing up a full diary of events that may or may not be used towards some further aim. Certainly it seems likely that there is more information buried in notebooks than ever sees the light of day in print, even in summary form.

For some, keeping a notebook is a chore, for others it is a delight. I have seen beautifully kept notebooks, neat and tidy with carefully entered names and numbers. Others are virtually essays written in the field, full of impressions and happenings. Many bird-watchers make sketches of birds, some representational showing the bird as it appeared in the field, others diagrammatical so that the diagnostic features can be shown as noted. Some watchers leave spaces for photographs to be added later, while Peter Scott's notebooks are full of superb paintings of the birds, fish and other animals that he observes on his travels. In his case the notebook is an art form in its own right.

My own notebooks, for what the information is worth, are basically lists of birds observed together with their numbers and sexes if appropriate. This basic structure is interrupted by names and addresses of people that I meet, a page or more of writing that summarises what I have learned of a particular place or bird, detailed plumage descriptions of birds that I have not seen before or which I am unable to identify at the time. Indeed anything that takes my fancy and seems worth recording. The result is an untidy hotch-potch, but one that I find incredibly useful.

I use a separate notebook for each major trip and find the 7 inches by 4½ inches hard-bound, lined, pocket-sized books available from all stationers ideal. I also use one or more for each year to cover my normal bird-watching in Britain. The result is a shelf full of identical books, but I write the date and locality on the spine for easy finding.

Whatever type of notebook you decide to keep, entries should follow a standard pattern and be set out under standard headings:

*Date, Time, Place, Weather, Companions*

*Access and Route*

*List of birds seen together with their numbers and sexes*

Many watchers use abbreviations, and 'c' for *circa* (meaning 'about') and ♂ for male and ♀ for female are in general use. There is, however, no reason why you should not devise

Wells Beach and Woods     Date: 29 October 1975
Weather: light wind from the east, small amount
           of cloud, mostly clear, but cold
Time: 10:00 — 11:30 hrs
Habitat: sandy estuary and woodland of
           pines, and birch with various bushes
Companions: J. Denton, P. Cooper, C. Mansell
50+ Redpolls                    2 Sanderling
♀ Blackcap                      1 Kestrel
10-15 Brent Geese               n. Tits, Goldcrests
2 Willow Tits              * 1 Yellow-browed Warbler

* Seen in area for last month. Regularly
fed in sallows on small undistinguishable
insects, and one brown caterpillar. Very active.
Small, "leaf" warbler, white underneath,
pinky brown legs, pale brown bill, lemon
green underparts, short tail, two pale wing-
bars, pale throat, dark green eyestripe, pale
lemon superciliary, darker top to head. Seen
for 5-10 minutes, call was loud 'seep' or
'sweet'. Associated with 'crests, good views

9. Page from a notebook.

your own provided that you keep them simple and can understand them yourself.

At the end of a day in the field it is often difficult to remember exactly what you have seen and while neat systematic lists are easier to use and refer to later, it is advisable to take a break from watching every now and again to get notes down while species and observations are fresh in the mind.

There are two useful methods of avoiding messing up a notebook in this way – a check-list or a tape recorder. Check lists of British birds and of European birds are published by the British Trust for Ornithology (BTO). They have spaces to tick off the birds seen as you go along and columns for five or so different days or trips. They cover all of the common birds and have space to write in the rarer ones that you are unlikely to forget anyway.

The new miniaturised tape recorders are so handy and cheap that they will doubtless become as useful to the field naturalist as they are to the hard-pressed businessman or politician. Birds can be recorded as they are seen, transcribed to your notebook in the evening and the tape left ready for use the following day.

## Noting a Bird

Notes on an unidentified bird can also be made on a tape recorder, though the discipline of a specially prepared form has distinct advantages for the beginner. The new bird is a great excitement and one that few of us ever grow out of. But if identification is to follow, a careful description is essential. If it is a rare bird you may wish to submit it to your local bird club or natural history society, or even to the Rarities Committee of *British Birds* magazine (see page 151). In each case an accurate field description will be required.

The first essential is to know something of the structure of a bird and what its various parts are called.

It is surprising how quickly one gets used to using these terms and armed with them a description actually begins to live for the reader. Try not to make your description too dry. If the bird is yellow all over, say so. If it is black and yellow, describe exactly which parts are yellow and which black. Be careful and be accurate, for a black patch in the wrong place might not seem important in England but in Africa among the various species of weavers it could lead to incorrect identification. Take particular notes of the presence or

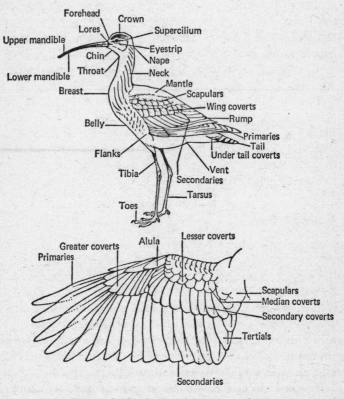

10. Parts of a bird named for easy reference.

absence of wing-bars, of rump patches, of the way the bird moves and flies, of its call notes and song, if any. Compare it with other birds present as well as similar species that are well known to you. Note the shape and length of its bill relative to the size of its head. Note what it was doing as exactly as possible; that is where it was, what sort of habitat it frequented and what food it took.

Though not intended to be perfect the following headings may guide your taking of notes on a problem bird:

1. Date, time, place.
2. Habitat.
3. What the bird was doing, e.g., flying, swimming, etc.
4. Size, preferably relative to another well-known species present at the same time.
5. General shape and impression, what sort of bird was it?
6. Coloration of upper parts, detailed description based on chart of bird's anatomy.
7. Underparts.
8. Bill – size, shape and colour.
9. Legs and feet, size and colour, i.e., do they trail behind the tail in flight?
10. Distinguishing features, wing-bars, etc.
11. Behaviour.
12. Call notes or song.
13. Identification.
14. How sure are you of your identification? In percentage form.

## Reports and Indexes

At the end of a bird-watching holiday you may wish to abstract your daily notes, pick out the more important items and put them into a more usable form. Hunting through a diary to see how many black-tailed godwits you saw in three weeks in North Africa can be a time-consuming job. The

best method is to write a check-list of species in the now
familiar Wetmore order. This is the order basically followed
in the field guides, and the one commonly used by bird-
watchers. It starts with the divers and ends with the crows
progressing from the more primitive to the more advanced
species. Work your way through your diary day by day
noting every significant observation of a species against
its name in the ordered check-list. Even while you are working a pattern may emerge which you were not aware of
before.

Some observers do the same thing in order to summarise
the results of their year of home-based bird-watching. This,
however, is less usual for it does not serve any useful purpose.
As an alternative they abstract from their notebook all
interesting observations within a particular area, usually a
county, so that they can be forwarded to the county or local
society for possible incorporation within the area report. An
element of rivalry enters this arena, for most local reports
follow observations of any merit by the observer's initials.
Thus the game of 'initialmanship' consists of doing better
than anyone else within a geographical area. It is a harmless
sport that can be fought on many fronts such as finding rare
migrants, seeking out unusual breeding birds, making
accurate censuses or counts of winter visitors and so on. Of
course such activity adds considerably to our knowledge of
birds in the area concerned, but even if it did not it would
still be good fun.

## Listing or Ticking

When we started watching birds almost all of us kept a list of
birds that we had seen. At first the total grew rapidly with
hardly a single field outing failing to add at least one new bird
to our list. We explored the birds of different seasons and
travelled about the country exploring different habitats.
Gradually, however, the list began to grow more slowly; we

continued seeing plenty of birds, but few were new to the list. At this point many bird-watchers abandon the whole business of ticking off birds and keeping a tally or life list. Nevertheless the desire to see a new bird is always there. It's a new one for the list, though the list may or may not actually be maintained. Some bird-watchers will travel hundreds of miles to see a new bird, whereas others will go no further than their local reservoir or marsh. It is only a matter of degree, for all of us are 'tickers' at heart.

Some watchers never get over the listing habit at all – they are often referred to as 'tick-hunters' or 'twitchers'. They are generally very keen and spend as much time as they can in the field searching for birds. Because they work so hard at it, they include some of the best identifiers of birds in the country. They have developed an expertise with the unusual bird by making it less unusual.

Though enlarging the life list is their primary aim they also invariably keep a year list as well. The advantage of this is that it keeps them chasing birds each year and every year, for a top twitcher might only have a chance of ten or so possible 'lifers' occurring in a twelve-month period. Naturally most of the twitchers know one another and have an unofficial red alert telephone news exchange system. A rare migrant might be seen by as many as twenty people the day after its discovery. But a hundred may be present on day three. If it stays around long enough the whole bird-watching fraternity will eventually get round to seeing it.

One aberrant thing about twitchers is that they never seem satisfied. They will return to see a rarity week-end after week-end, thus building up their familiarity with the species. They will also seek out a rarity that they had seen earlier in the year so as to compare one individual with another.

The champion tick-hunter is my friend Ron Johns who, like most twitchers, lives and works in a large city. His life list in Britain and Ireland was over 380 by mid-1975 and he achieved his big year in 1967 when he saw 297 separate species. During the twelve months he covered over 40,000 miles by road and a substantial number in the air.

In North America tickers are known as 'listers', but this is not the only difference. Listing is significantly more respectable on the other side of the Atlantic: indeed almost every bird-watcher is a lister. A significant proportion belong to the American Birding Association (ABA) including all the big names like Peterson and Robbins, the authors of the standard, and competitive, field guides. There is much competition between members and their magazine *Birding* devotes much space to collections of annual totals and life lists. Useful inserts in the magazine show exactly how to find the rarer American birds with instructions almost down to the 'which bush' level. This picks out an interesting difference between the situations on either side of the Atlantic, for while egg-collectors (so called oologists) are an ever-present threat to a rare British bird, there is no such danger facing American birds. Another difference, and one that I personally find such an appealing part of British bird-watching, is the high percentage of vagrants that have found their way to these islands. Literally one just does not know what will turn up next.

The ABA records include 626 species in a year within the American Ornithologists' Union Checklist area by Ted Parker III in 1971. In 1972 Joe Taylor of New York State became the first to break the 700 life list barrier. Several American birders have managed to amass life lists of over ninety per cent of the possible birds for the state in which they live. Thus Tom Imhof has seen 337 species in Alabama, a figure which represents no less than ninety-six per cent of that State's total. Unfortunately there is no similar organisation over here, though unofficial figures are circulated among the twitchers themselves.

Before anyone compares tick-hunting with train spotting, I would point out that all of the birds seen must satisfy the observer as to their correct identification, and that is a lot more difficult than noting a passing number. Identifying birds is a great skill and one that, with practice, can become a full time hobby on its own account.

## Clubs and Societies

The British are great club formers and joiners and virtually no part of the country remains uncovered by one bird society or another. Most of these are based on the old county system of political boundaries, though some are more local covering only a few parishes while others are composites dealing with birds in areas like large cities. Many of the societies cover all aspects of natural history, while others are more specifically concerned with birds. Addresses, which change as frequently as the honorary secretary, can be obtained from the local library.

Most societies organise field meetings during the summer and indoor meetings through the winter. Some are enterprising and some are not. Field meetings may consist of a walk round a local wood, or a day (even weekend) coach trip to an outstanding bird resort. Some societies even organise their own overseas holidays, though this is unusual compared with the situation in the United States. Field meetings are excellent for getting to know members and seeing new places and birds. The leader invariably knows the area to be visited very well and it is worth sticking close to him.

Indoor meetings invariably consist of an invited speaker who will be popular if he shows his own film, successful if he shows slides of birds, and ill-attended if he talks about science. Other business is also conducted and gives an opportunity for new members to introduce themselves to the club's officers. The RSPB is becoming increasingly influential in local bird-watching and its local group scheme organises indoor and field meetings for members living within range. Sometimes these are held in conjunction with local societies, but in other areas the local RSPB group is self-sufficient. The RSPB also has a flourishing junior section called the Young Ornithologists' Club (YOC). It issues a magazine, holds meetings and introduces young bird-watchers (under the age of eighteen years) to local experts who are prepared to take them out and get them into bird-watching. Scientific overtones are minimal and there is no doubt that joining the YOC is a sound start to becoming a bird-watcher. Certainly most bird-watchers belong to a local society or group of some sort.

Societies, like everything else, vary in quality. They are dependent for their success, or lack of it, on the people who run them. Before you join and part with money, ask to go along to one of their field meetings. If they do not have any, look elsewhere for your club. Also attend an indoor meeting if you can (most good societies will be only too willing to give you a free sample) and judge for yourself whether it is the sort of organisation that you are looking for.

## How to Watch Birds

So far we have covered the bird-watcher's equipment, his library, his notebooks and record keeping, listing and ticking, societies and clubs, but have said nothing about the art of watching birds itself. It may be argued that watching birds is like plumbing – it cannot be learned from a book or an evening class, but only in the doing. No doubt there is much truth in this assertion, but I believe that some hints on field-craft are worth noting.

Dress is optional, and must be suited to the conditions. But while most birds will see you before you see them, there is no need to advertise your presence by wearing bright reds and yellows when you could more easily merge with the background in greens and browns. Most watchers have one of those ex-army parkas in dull green to keep out the cold during a howling nor'easter on winter coasts and estuaries. Warm pullovers, gloves and Wellington boots are all essentials for the British bird-watcher. Abroad, and in the summer, lighter clothes are needed, but always keep the colours sombre.

Watching birds is often a matter of going for a walk with binoculars, but it is not the only way to do it. The successful watcher actively searches for his birds. He explores an area for prime bird habitat; he knows the types of birds he will find in each. He will time his trips to maximise his chances of seeing whatever he wants to see. But above all he will search.

If he finds a marsh with a few waders he will sit down out of the wind with the sun shining over his shoulder and pick out each bird one by one, making correct identification before he passes on to the next. He will scan every nook and cranny with his binoculars to see what he has missed, and certainly wait for a while to see what will materialise. Perhaps an interesting bird will emerge from cover, perhaps a rare bird will fly in while he watches.

At a promontory or on an island where migrants are regularly present some bird-watchers will rush around like wild things expecting rare birds to appear around every turn. The more experienced (and that is not a function simply of age) will seek out the best spot and concentrate their attentions on it for long periods. After a while one gets a feeling about places – that they will be good or no good for migrants. When birds alight during their travels they head for the nearest shelter and food. With waders or duck it is easy to spot likely places on a map, but with small birds you may be on the right island but in the wrong place.

If you find a few bushes sheltered from the wind in a dip and with a few common migrants present, settle down for a while to see what happens. Watch the sunny side, because in the early mornings (and I do mean early) birds like to come out and dry themselves in the sun. Others may be thrashing about all over the place, but sit and watch carefully and satisfy yourself that you have seen every bird in the clump before moving on to search for another likely spot. Along the

East Bank at Cley, a great meeting place, bird-watchers may be found lounging and chatting almost idly by mid-morning. What the disapproving late-comers do not realise is that most of them have been up since before dawn and will have worked the area for hours while others lay abed.

Of course some birds will come your way as you stroll along, and the more hours you put in the field searching the better you should do. Companions are also useful, and while most Radde's warblers (a rare Asiatic species much sought after in late autumn) will disappear completely as the 52-seater coach decants the Kensington Bird Watching and Rambling Club on its annual outing, two or three pairs of eyes will find more birds than one. Search the bushes then, do not beat them. Sit and watch quietly, do not run around intent on covering as much ground as possible. Maximise your chances of success by looking, and not just in front of you. One bird-watcher I know jokingly keeps a list of birds that have seen him without him seeing them. He is the only man I know who has been seen by a gyr falcon but has not got that bird on his life list.

Have your binoculars ready and pre-focused to the distance you are searching. Birds at a distance usually remain in view for some time, but a nearby warbler may appear and disappear before you have time to focus. Use your binoculars to search for birds, do not rely on the naked eye to pick them up and leave the binoculars for closer views. Scan a thicket and you will be surprised to find birds that you would otherwise have missed.

Keep your ears open too and investigate every unknown sound. This may be a time-consuming business, for at first they will all turn out to be commonplace species. But the effort of searching reinforces the memory and makes it more likely that you will remember the sound and not have to investigate it again on another trip. You may, of course, aid this process with recordings of bird voices at home.

Sea-watching is a sport in its own right and it is surprising what a misty morning on a prominent headland can produce. As a time-consuming passion for bird-watchers it only really began to gain popularity in the early 1960s. Now it is a regular occupation of all keen field-men. Find a prominent watch point (height above the sea is important) and then a sheltered place out of the wind. Scan the sea carefully and then do it again with binoculars. An hour is usually sufficient to tell whether or not a sea-watch is going to be productive or not. Telescopes really come into their own with this sort of watching and one firmly mounted on a tripod is an exceedingly valuable tool. Of course you will be lucky to get really close views of birds and your identification will depend on recognising characteristic plumage patterns and manners of flight. Most field guides are not very useful in this respect.

Finding birds is then an activity, and not simply a matter of going for walks on the off-chance that they might come your way. Think, plan and search is the sequence for anyone who wants to find his own birds.

From time to time you will hear of rare birds through the grapevine. The more active you become and the more people you meet the more information you will receive. Chase off after them and you will meet even more people, thus extending your contacts, and perhaps see a new bird as well. Ticking off a bird found by someone else is never as satisfying as finding your own, but it is the bird that counts and familiarity with a new British species becomes progressively more difficult as your life list mounts.

## Bird Photography

Photographing birds is a subject on its own which has occupied several books. I attempted to deal with it in a single chapter in *Wildlife Photography* (Hutchinson, London) which I wrote jointly with Eric Hosking. I shall not attempt to summarise here. Photographing birds is a field sport and a valuable one at that. With a camera you may photograph a bird's eggs and nest, record an aspect of its behaviour, or simply obtain a portrait. Today more bird-watchers than ever carry cameras and most are equipped with telephoto lenses of varying focal lengths. With a little care and patience they could get some great pictures: instead they end up with thousands of blurred and soft transparencies. These transparencies may, however, serve their purpose and may even project quite well, but most would be thrown away by the more serious photographers as just so much rubbish.

If bird photography appeals to you, read a book before you spend a lot of money on unsuitable equipment. Listen to your friends by all means; but still read a book. The problem revolves around the length of lens required to snap at birds, and the speed of modern colour film. The slower the film the better the definition of the processed transparency, but to catch a small active thing like a bird you need a fast shutter speed and herein lies the contradiction – the bird-photographer's dilemma.

Fast shutter speed and slow film just do not go together. Most action photographers go for a faster and more grainy film, whereas most of the professionals settle for the slower

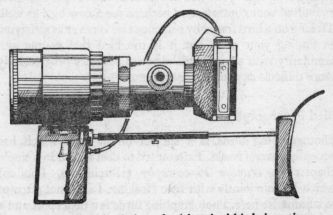

11. The shoulder-holster for 'shooting' birds in action.

film and risk the chances of blur due to subject movement. Their film wastage is high, but the results are crisp, very crisp indeed.

In recent years bird photography has become emancipated from the nest and hide situation. Modern 35 mm cameras are highly refined pieces of machinery and the range of interchangeable lenses offers something that is ideal for almost every circumstance. Many are cheap and, though you get what you pay for, a reasonable outfit is not beyond the means of most people. Long lenses enable the photographer to contemplate shots by the stalking method that were quite unthinkable even fifteen years ago. Indeed there has developed a new artistry in bird-photography, and the new masters obtain action shots of immense interest. Rarities at sewage works, duck in flight, birds fighting, all are now taken by the action men. As yet there are few masters, but there will be more.

# CHAPTER THREE

# When to Watch Birds

Successful bird-watching is the art of knowing where and when to look for what. Birds can be found everywhere, and even unusual species have the knack of turning up in the most extraordinary places. Bitterns have been seen in the streets of London, a stone curlew dropped into a children's sandpit (its natural, if confused, habitat) and a tiny sewage bed near my London home produced greenshank and wood sandpiper. Most bird-watchers have found their own good places, places that produce unusual birds. Indeed a glance at a map will often be sufficient to tell the experienced watcher where he should go. Some birds will, on occasion, break the rules and turn up in unlikely places at unusual times of the year, but most birds are regular creatures of habit and appear only at certain places at certain times.

A guide to bird seasons is of crucial importance to all watchers. It is as pointless looking for a reed warbler in January as it is looking for a shorelark in June. The best seasons are spring and autumn, for it is at this time that migration brings a host of birds to our shores that neither breed nor winter with us. Spring is the season of the arrival of summer visitors, though winter visitors may linger to make up those interesting juxtapositions of species that add spice to our watching. Autumn passage is generally heavier with all the young birds of the year setting out on their first journeys. It is these younger birds that have the greatest propensity to wander and autumn is thus the best season for off-course vagrants. It is the top season at the bird observatories and migration watch points, when all the beds are booked months in advance.

Unfortunately not all birds have the same sense of season as we do. Some are earlier in spring than others, and while winter for fieldfares starts in October the white-fronted geese do not arrive in southern England until after Christmas. The fact that birds' seasons vary so much is one of their fascinations, but it is also of extreme value to bird-watchers. Know the seasons and you are prepared for what to expect.

## A bird-watcher's calendar

The calendar which follows makes no allowance between southern England and northern Scotland, a distance of some 700 miles. There is a difference of ten degrees of latitude between Lands End and southern Shetland, and that makes a significant difference in timing.

APRIL sees the first arrivals of most summer visitors. Though wheatears and chiffchaffs may be flitting around the south coast in late March, few others arrive until the end of the first week of April. Then willow warblers begin to trickle through and the first cuckoo is reported. Late April sees swallows in numbers and shorebirds begin to build up on the estuaries.

MAY is the main arrival month, with most of the summer visitors really becoming obvious. Early swifts may be hawking overhead by 28th April, but they are uncommon well into May. Red-backed shrikes arrive and numbers of waders build up to a mid-month peak. The 15th May is traditionally 'Godwit Day' in Suffolk. If black terns are going to turn up, 12th to 15th May is the best spring period. Many resident species have already reared one brood.

JUNE is the breeding month when most of our summer visitors are nesting. Some stragglers continue to arrive and fine weather may produce a few strays from the south that have overshot their usual range. Little egret, hoopoe and golden oriole are examples and the latter two sometimes stay on to breed. This is the month to visit the seabird colonies with which Britain and Ireland are so well endowed, and the Scottish Highlands for their unique bird fauna. Bird photographers are exposing reel upon reel of film and tick hunters are adding the rarer breeders to their life lists.

JULY is traditionally a quiet month for birds and bird-watchers. But there are plenty of birds to be seen breeding and there is the first flush of migrant summer visitors during the last week of the month. These include such diverse birds as warblers in the London parks and terns along the coasts.

AUGUST sees migration really getting under way. Observatories gather their warblers by the hundreds while the fresh marshes become alive with the best collection of waders of the year. Spotted redshanks, little stints and curlew sandpipers, all are present in varying numbers along with greenshanks and the fine black terns. Sea terns flock along the coasts, heads down for the south. The latter part of August and the whole of September is rarity time, the time when unusual birds are most likely to occur. Their arrival does not coincide with the peak of passage, for many species occur later. Bluethroat, wryneck, barred warbler, Temminck's stint, pectoral sandpiper, pomarine skua, Cory's and sooty shearwaters – these are the birds of this exciting period.

SEPTEMBER sees the gradual disappearance of one species after another. Watch out for the last of the swifts and the first of the fieldfares. Rarities are everywhere and tick hunters have a difficult choice every weekend. Most will head for the east coast south of Durham hoping for one of those spectacular falls of migrants that can be one of the most thrilling experiences of a British bird-watcher's lifetime. This is also a peak month for American waders: trans-Atlantic passerines tend to come later, in October.

OCTOBER is a migration month too, and though numbers may be smaller there are rarities about that do not occur earlier. Siberian birds are most notable and yellow-browed and greenish warblers can be a daily occurrence at the more favourably sited spots. This is the month of diurnal migrants and birds can be seen following the coastline in flock after flock. These movements can also be seen inland along a range of hills and even over large cities. Immigrant robins create havoc among resident birds and fieldfares and redwings gather to feast along the hedgerows. In a good season an irruption of crossbills or waxwings may occur and in the west sea-watching can produce Sabine's gulls.

NOVEMBER tends to be rather quiet in comparison. There may be large arrivals of fieldfares and redwings at the beginning, and a chance of 'wrecks' of seabirds with north-westerly gales throughout the month. Geese arrive *en masse* in the north and winter wader populations build up along the shoreline.

DECEMBER is, in general, a stable month with all the usual birds settled in their winter quarters. Great grey shrikes, siskins, bramblings and rough-legged buzzards may be found.

JANUARY usually sees the first of the hard weather and with it come geese and Bewick's swans to southern England, while duck populations build up to a maximum. Unusual northern gulls occur and divers form flocks at favoured spots along the coasts.

FEBRUARY is the peak month for wildfowl, and reservoirs and marshes are the major haunts of bird-watchers.

Sometimes sea-duck like scoter and long-tailed duck appear inland, but in general few new species occur.

MARCH brings the first signs of spring. Many winter visitors depart and the first of the summer migrants, the wheatears and chiffchaffs, arrive before the month is through.

Thus we come full circle and set off once more in search of the summer visitors that so occupy the April scene. From the calendar it is possible to work out a week by week strategy for seeing birds in this country. With some travelling it is possible to see 200 species in a year without too much trouble, and with 200 comes a broad understanding of the British avifauna.

## Bird Seasons

The 'when' factor then depends on the bird's internal clock system and its established pattern of seasonal behaviour. For convenience birds may be divided into a number of handy categories: Resident and Breeds (RB): Summer Visitor and Breeds (SB): Passage Migrant (PM): Winter Visitor (WV): Rarity (R). Naturally such categories are not in any way mutually exclusive. Thus the robin is a resident breeder, but some of our birds migrate and are thus summer visitors. Many Scandinavian robins migrate to winter in this country and are thus winter visitors, while some pass onwards and are thus passage migrants. Thus the Robin falls into four of the five categories of British birds. Similar patterns obtain for many others. In the list that follows the more common birds are summarised and the majority of rarities excluded.

### Seasonal Status of British Birds

| Great northern diver | WV |
| Black-throated diver | RB, WV |

| | |
|---|---|
| Red-throated diver | RB, SB, WV |
| Great crested grebe | RB, WV |
| Red-necked grebe | WV |
| Slavonian grebe | RB, WV, PM |
| Black-necked grebe | RB, WV, PM |
| Little grebe | RB, WV |
| Fulmar | RB, SB |
| Manx shearwater | SB, PM |
| Great shearwater | PM |
| Sooty shearwater | PM |
| Cory's shearwater | PM |
| Storm petrel | SB, PM |
| Leach's petrel | SB, PM |
| Gannet | RB, SB, PM |
| Shag | RB, SB, WV |
| Cormorant | RB, SB, WV, PM |
| Grey heron | RB, SB, WV, PM |
| Bittern | RB, WV |
| Spoonbill | PM |
| Mute swan | RB, SB, WV |
| Whooper swan | WV |
| Bewick's swan | WV |
| Greylag goose | RB, WV |
| Bean goose | WV |
| Pink-footed goose | WV |
| White-fronted goose | WV |
| Brent goose | WV |
| Barnacle goose | WV |
| Canada goose | RB |
| Shelduck | RB, SB, WV |
| Mallard | RB, SB, WV, PM |
| Gadwall | RB, SB, WV |
| Wigeon | RB, WV, PM |
| Teal | RB, SB, WV, PM |
| Garganey | SB, PM |
| Pintail | RB, WV, PM |

| | |
|---|---|
| Shoveler | RB, SB, WV, PM |
| Red-crested pochard | PM |
| Tufted duck | RB, WV, PM |
| Scaup | WV, PM |
| Pochard | RB, WV, PM |
| Eider | RB, WV |
| Scoter | RB, WV, PM |
| Velvet scoter | WV, PM |
| Goldeneye | WV, PM |
| Long-tailed duck | WV |
| Goosander | RB, WV |
| Red-breasted merganser | RB, WV |
| Smew | WV |
| Osprey | SB, PM |
| Red kite | RB |
| Sparrowhawk | RB, WV, PM |
| Buzzard | RB, PM |
| Rough-legged buzzard | WV, PM |
| Honey buzzard | SB |
| Golden eagle | RB |
| Marsh harrier | RB, SB, WV, PM |
| Hen harrier | RB, SB, WV, PM |
| Montagu's harrier | SB, PM |
| Peregrine | RB, WV, PM |
| Hobby | SB, PM |
| Merlin | RB, SB, WV, PM |
| Kestrel | RB, SB, WV, PM |
| Red grouse | RB |
| Ptarmigan | RB |
| Black grouse | RB |
| Capercaillie | RB |
| Red-legged partridge | RB |
| Grey partridge | RB |
| Quail | SB |
| Ring-necked pheasant | RB |
| Golden pheasant | RB |

| | |
|---|---|
| Lady Amherst's pheasant | RB |
| Water rail | RB, WV, PM |
| Spotted crake | SB, PM |
| Corncrake | SB, PM |
| Moorhen | RB, WV |
| Coot | RB, WV |
| Oystercatcher | RB, SB, WV, PM |
| Avocet | SB, WV, PM |
| Ringed plover | RB, SB, WV, PM |
| Little ringed plover | SB |
| Golden plover | RB, SB, WV, PM |
| Grey plover | WV, PM |
| Dotterel | SB, PM |
| Turnstone | WV, PM |
| Lapwing | RB, SB, WV, PM |
| Curlew sandpiper | PM |
| Dunlin | RB, SB, WV, PM |
| Temminck's stint | PM |
| Little stint | PM |
| Knot | WV, PM |
| Sanderling | WV, PM |
| Purple sandpiper | WV, PM |
| Grey phalarope | PM |
| Red-necked phalarope | SB, PM |
| Redshank | RB, SB, WV, PM |
| Spotted redshank | PM |
| Greenshank | SB, PM, WV |
| Common sandpiper | SB, PM |
| Wood sandpiper | SB, PM |
| Green sandpiper | PM |
| Ruff | SB, WV, PM |
| Curlew | RB, SB, WV, PM |
| Whimbrel | SB, PM |
| Black-tailed godwit | SB, WV, PM |
| Bar-tailed godwit | WV, PM |
| Woodcock | RB, SB, WV, PM |

| | |
|---|---|
| Jack snipe | WV, PM |
| Snipe | RB, SB, WV, PM |
| Stone curlew | SB |
| Great skua | SB, PM |
| Arctic skua | SB, PM |
| Long-tailed skua | PM |
| Pomarine skua | PM |
| Black-headed gull | RB, SB, WV, PM |
| Little gull | PM |
| Mediterranean gull | PM |
| Sabine's gull | PM |
| Herring gull | RB, SB, WV |
| Lesser black-backed gull | SB, WV, PM |
| Great black-backed gull | RB, SB, WV |
| Glaucous gull | WV |
| Iceland gull | WV |
| Common gull | RB, SB, WV, PM |
| Kittiwake | RB, SB, WV, PM |
| Sandwich tern | SB, PM |
| Common tern | SB, PM |
| Arctic tern | SB, PM |
| Roseate tern | SB, PM |
| Little tern | SB, PM |
| Black tern | PM |
| Razorbill | RB, SB, WV |
| Guillemot | RB, SB, WV |
| Puffin | RB, SB, WV |
| Black guillemot | RB |
| Little auk | PM |
| Rock dove | RB |
| Stock dove | RB, SB, WV, PM |
| Wood pigeon | RB, SB, WV |
| Collared dove | RB |
| Turtle dove | SB, PM |
| Cuckoo | SB, PM |
| Barn owl | RB |

| | |
|---|---|
| Snowy owl | RB, R |
| Long-eared owl | RB, WV, PM |
| Short-eared owl | RB, SB, WV, PM |
| Little owl | RB |
| Tawny owl | RB |
| Nightjar | SB |
| Swift | SB, PM |
| Kingfisher | RB |
| Hoopoe | PM |
| Green woodpecker | RB |
| Great spotted woodpecker | RB, WV |
| Lesser spotted woodpecker | RB |
| Wryneck | SB, PM |
| Shorelark | WV |
| Woodlark | RB |
| Skylark | RB, WV, PM |
| Swallow | SB, PM |
| Sand martin | SB, PM |
| House martin | SB, PM |
| Tree pipit | SB, PM |
| Meadow pipit | RB, SB, WV, PM |
| Rock/water pipit | RB, WV, PM |
| Pied/white wagtail | RB, SB, PM |
| Grey wagtail | RB, SB, PM |
| Yellow wagtail | SB, PM |
| Waxwing | WV |
| Great grey shrike | WV, PM |
| Red-backed shrike | SB, PM |
| Dunnock | RB, WV, PM |
| Grasshopper warbler | SB, PM |
| Savi's warbler | SB |
| Reed warbler | SB, PM |
| Marsh warbler | SB |
| Sedge warbler | SB, PM |
| Cetti's warbler | SB |
| Icterine warbler | PM |

| | |
|---|---|
| Melodious warbler | R |
| Whitethroat | SB, PM |
| Lesser whitethroat | SB, PM |
| Garden warbler | SB, PM |
| Barred warbler | PM |
| Blackcap | SB, WV, PM |
| Dartford warbler | RB |
| Willow warbler | SB, PM |
| Chiffchaff | SB, WV, PM |
| Wood warbler | SB, PM |
| Goldcrest | RB, WV, PM |
| Firecrest | SB, WV, PM |
| Spotted flycatcher | SB, PM |
| Pied flycatcher | SB, PM |
| Stonechat | RB, SB, PM |
| Whinchat | SB, PM |
| Wheatear | SB, PM |
| Black redstart | SB, WV, PM |
| Redstart | SB, PM |
| Robin | RB, SB, WV, PM |
| Bluethroat | PM |
| Nightingale | SB |
| Blackbird | RB, SB, WV, PM |
| Ring ouzel | SB, PM |
| Fieldfare | WV, PM |
| Redwing | WV, PM |
| Song thrush | RB, SB, WV, PM |
| Mistle thrush | RB, SB |
| Bearded tit | RB, WV |
| Long-tailed tit | RB |
| Coal tit | RB |
| Great tit | RB, WV |
| Blue tit | RB, WV |
| Crested tit | RB |
| Marsh tit | RB |
| Willow tit | RB |

| | |
|---|---|
| Nuthatch | RB |
| Tree creeper | RB |
| Wren | RB |
| Dipper | RB, WV |
| Corn bunting | RB |
| Yellowhammer | RB |
| Cirl bunting | RB |
| Ortolan bunting | PM |
| Reed bunting | RB, WV, PM |
| Snow bunting | RB, WV, PM |
| Lapland bunting | WV, PM |
| Brambling | WV, PM |
| Chaffinch | RB, WV, PM |
| Goldfinch | RB, SB |
| Siskin | RB, WV, PM |
| Greenfinch | RB, SB, WV, PM |
| Bullfinch | RB |
| Hawfinch | RB |
| Redpoll | RB, SB, WV, PM |
| Twite | RB, SB, WV |
| Linnet | RB, SB, WV |
| Serin | SB |
| Crossbill | RB, WV |
| Tree sparrow | RB, WV |
| House sparrow | RB |
| Starling | RB, SB, WV, PM |
| Jay | RB, WV |
| Magpie | RB |
| Chough | RB |
| Raven | RB |
| Rook | RB, WV |
| Carrion crow | RB, WV |
| Jackdaw | RB, WV |

(After British Ornithologists' Union,
*The Status of Birds in Britain and Ireland, Blackwell*)

Unfortunately a table like this is quite unable to distinguish between different seasons for different birds. For example the crossbill, while classified as a resident breeder, in fact breeds in January so that it can feed its young on the seeds of the opening pine cones. The autumn passage period extends from late July through August, September, October into November. Within this period some species are early migrants like swifts while others are late like fieldfares. Absolute earliest and latest dates are comparatively useless, but Robert Hudson has produced a useful guide published by the BTO giving the fifteen earliest and latest reports of fifty common summer visitors. It is an invaluable guide and a selection of the more interesting species is given here. In each case the fifteenth earliest and fifteenth latest date recorded up until 1973 is given. This gives some idea of the extreme rarity of birds before and after those dates, as well as indicating to anyone who observes an out of season bird whether or not it is worth reporting. It also indicates the dates between which birds may be looked for in Britain.

### Early and Late Summer Migrants

| | | |
|---|---|---|
| Garganey | 26 February | –  6 December |
| Montagu's harrier | 28 March | –  7 November |
| Osprey | 23 March | – 22 November |
| Hobby | 31 March | –  6 November |
| Little ringed plover | 21 March | – 20 October |
| Wood sandpiper | 9 April | – 11 November |
| Red-necked phalarope | 15 May | – 21 November |
| Stone curlew | 5 March | –  1 December |
| Black tern | 9 April | – 12 November |
| Common tern | 22 March | – 26 November |
| Arctic tern | 12 April | –  5 November |
| Little tern | 8 April | – 31 October |
| Sandwich tern | 12 March | – 16 November |
| Turtle dove | 28 March | – 26 November |

| | | |
|---|---|---|
| Cuckoo | 24 March | – 10 November |
| Nightjar | 15 April | – 27 October |
| Swift | 4 April | – 17 November |
| Wryneck | 14 March | – 25 October |
| Swallow | 25 February | – 24 December |
| House martin | 8 March | – 20 December |
| Sand martin | 8 March | – 28 November |
| Ring ouzel | 21 February | – 10 December |
| Wheatear | 19 February | – 9 December |
| Whinchat | 17 March | – 25 November |
| Redstart | 20 March | – 15 November |
| Nightingale | 2 April | – 4 October |
| Grasshopper warbler | 5 April | – 16 October |
| Reed warbler | 7 April | – 29 October |
| Sedge warbler | 26 March | – 27 October |
| Garden warbler | 1 April | – 16 November |
| Whitethroat | 25 March | – 15 November |
| Lesser whitethroat | 7 April | – 12 November |
| Willow warbler | 8 March | – 24 November |
| Wood warbler | 4 April | – 30 September |
| Spotted flycatcher | 9 April | – 29 October |
| Pied flycatcher | 8 April | – 30 October |
| Tree pipit | 21 March | – 25 October |
| Yellow wagtail | 19 March | – 8 December |
| Red-backed shrike | 15 April | – 23 October |

(After R. Hudson, *BTO Guide No. 15*)

## Migration Influences

No aspect of the life of birds is so fascinating as their migrations. This is particularly true in Britain, where such a large
proportion of our birds are regular migrants or vagrants. The
British Isles, only narrowly separated from a continental
land-mass, are ideally situated to gather in the unusual. The
regular migration route from Scandinavia crosses the

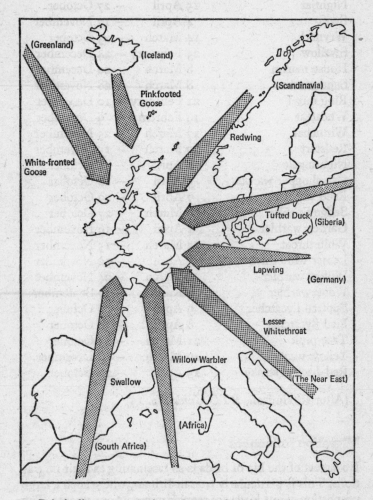

**12.** Britain lies at a great interchange of birds and draws species from almost every direction.

southern part of the country for birds that migrate south-westwards towards Iberia. Birds following the continental coast of the North Sea regularly fly the Channel from Cap Gris Nez, where the coast turns sharply southwards. Sea-birds moving to and from the Arctic Ocean, like World War II battleships, must pass between the Shetlands and Iceland, and inevitably some are blown onshore in the north-west. The warm Gulf Stream flows across the Atlantic from the eastern coasts of the United States bringing with it flocks of shearwaters and petrels that can be seen in the extreme south-west of these islands. While any American waif that finds itself drifted out over the Atlantic might well seek a suitable landing place in western Britain. All of these various influences have a profound effect on the British List of birds.

## Summer Visitors

Summer visitors to Britain arrive from two main directions. Most species come from the south-west while a few like the red-backed shrike and lesser whitethroat arrive from the south-east. Many passerine birds make huge journeys involving crossing the Mediterranean and the Sahara in one non-stop flight, perhaps the most formidable barrier on earth regularly navigated by birds. These birds move on a broad front and not along narrow corridors or flight lines. Untold numbers die along the way, but the advantage to the species as a whole offsets the loss. Some species move no further than southern Europe, others cross the Mediterranean–Saharan barrier, but then stop to winter in the Sahel belt along the southern edge of the desert. The whitethroat is a case in point, and the catastrophic decline in numbers of this species in recent years has been linked with the increasing aridity of the Sahel that has brought famine to the nomadic tribes that live there. Others move further south into the West African rainforests and East African savannahs, while our swallows progress southwards as far as they can, to the Cape of Good Hope. Each population of European swallows has a quite distinct wintering zone. Thus German swallows are found in quite different regions from those bred in Britain.

While swallows migrate by day, many other species are basically nocturnal migrants. Thus counting swallows passing a migration watchpoint is a pleasant autumn pastime, whereas those who would see nocturnal migrants must be up at first light searching the bushes.

Diurnal migrants navigate by the sun while nocturnal species utilise the stars. Both have internal clocks; but while the general position of the sun is only seldom totally obscured, a cloudy night completely blocks off the stars from view. On such nights nocturnal migrants will not set off. But sometimes the sky is clear at their point of origin and obscured by cloud along the way. In these circumstances large numbers of birds are totally disorientated and may end up miles off course. During nights like this hundreds of birds may be attracted by the beams of light thrown out by lighthouses – any port in a storm. Formerly many died as they dashed themselves against the glass of the lamp. Now most lighthouses are floodlit and, though birds still follow the beam, they can see the lighthouse itself when they get close and avoid killing themselves.

If birds become disorientated during the night they will frequently alight at the nearest coast in large numbers soon after dawn. This phenomenon is called a 'fall'. Falls are particularly likely to occur on our east coast with migrants of Scandinavian origin. Typically they consist of willow warblers and pied flycatchers together with a sprinkling of blue-throats and wrynecks. It is tantalising to think of the vast numbers of these birds that pass straight over us without alighting during normal clear weather.

Another class of summer migrants that provoke some interest are the passerine rarities like the red-breasted flycatcher and Arctic warblers that appear every autumn, but whose migration routes should lead them directly away from us. The explanation seems to be either that juveniles of these species explode in all manner of directions at the end of the breeding season and before they set off on migration for winter quarters, or that they follow a path directly opposite to their normal migration route. The latter, the usually

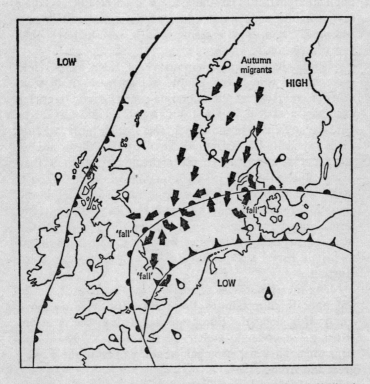

13. Typical weather situation leading to an east coast 'fall' of migrants. Clear skies over Scandinavia prompt night migrants to set out, but they soon encounter a warm front over the North Sea and are disorientated beneath the clouds. The result – a heavy arrival of tired migrants along the nearest coasts.

accepted explanation, is referred to as reverse migration. In either case this may well bring them to our shores to the delight of any bird-watcher fortunate enough to come across them. Even stranger is the arrival of birds that breed as far away as eastern Siberia. Pallas's and Radde's warblers fall into this category and are among the most sought-after of rarities. Perhaps their journeys are prompted by high population densities at the end of a successful breeding season in the same way as the irruptions of crossbills and waxwings begin. Such extreme rarities are usually October east coast birds.

Seabirds have migration patterns of their own. While some species would seem simply to disperse over the seas, others have quite definite migration routes. Arctic terns, for example, cross the Atlantic from Greenland and Canada to join the stream of Scandinavian and British birds working their way along the Atlantic coasts. Together they continue along the west coast of Africa to the Antarctic where they winter among the pack ice. At some time in the distant past, part of the population of this species established itself in the south to breed and became a separate species – the Antarctic tern. Arctic terns migrate 22,000 miles a year, or twice the distance covered by the average family car. Two birds ringed in Britain have been recovered as far away as south-eastern Australia.

Manx shearwaters also regularly cross the Atlantic, but in the opposite direction to the terns. British birds move southwards along the European and African coasts before crossing the ocean to winter off the coasts of Brazil and Argentina. They are accompanied at least part of the way by great and Arctic skuas.

Undoubtedly Britain's greatest claim to international fame lies in her seabird colonies. Almost every cliff supports some seabirds while those of the north and west hold some of the most exciting seabird colonies to be found anywhere. While peak activity is during May and June, many seabirds return to their cliffs very early to ensure their tenancy of a good nest site. Fulmars are back on the ledges by November while guillemots return soon after Christmas. Thus the cliffs are deserted only from August through to the end of the year – a mere four months.

## Winter Visitors

Just as the summer visitors leave us to seek milder climes for the winter, so do birds that breed further north move southwards to winter with us. Some of these are passerines, but the vast majority are wetland birds, waders and wildfowl, that find along our highly tidal and indented coastline ample food and safety.

Waders are extraordinarily numerous around our shores and recent counts have shown that as many as 1,400,000 birds find these islands a happy winter home. Certainly a significant proportion of the total European wader population winters in Britain including no less than seventy per cent of Europe's knot and roughly half of the continent's dunlin, redshank, curlew and bar-tailed godwits. Birds in such numbers offer spectacular bird-watching to any willing to brave the winter estuaries. Some species, however, are very localised in winter and only the watcher who knows where to go will find avocets, greenshanks, little stints or ruff.

Flocks of wildfowl are comparatively commonplace and seaduck can be found all around our coasts. Inland almost every lowland reservoir holds duck, some in very large numbers. Scanning a flock with a telescope is an exciting business, not only because of the opportunity of spotting an unusual bird, but for the sheer joy of seeing so many birds packed together.

Geese and wild swans are more local in their distribution particularly in the south. In Scotland it's a poor loch that does not boast a few greylags and whoopers, but in England they are concentrated at a few traditional wintering sites.

White-fronts at Slimbridge, Bewick's swans on the Ouse
Washes, bean geese in an unmentionable part of Norfolk,
brent at Wells-next-the-Sea, these are the top places to see
these fine winter visitors.

Winter is also a good time for gulls, and many watchers
now devote considerable time to searching for the more
unusual species. Glaucous and Iceland gulls may turn up
anywhere, but are more numerous in the north. Indeed
glaucous gulls are nearly always to be found at this season in
Lerwick Harbour. Single Mediterranean gulls frequently
return to winter every year at the same spot and may appear
for as many as ten successive winters. The Arctic based gulls,
ivory and Ross's, are extreme rarities, but may be worth
searching for by the sea among the largest gull flocks during
the most severe part of the winter.

Passerine winter visitors are generally widespread with
fieldfares, redwings, siskins and bramblings covering the
country. How many there are of them we do not know. Snow
buntings in contrast are essentially east coast birds and
usually appear from October onwards in small to medium-
sized flocks. Other flocks can be found on the hills of Scotland among which a few pairs remain to breed. Shorelarks
are rarer and even more confined to the east coast.

## Birds of Passage

Passage migrants hold a special attraction for the birds
watcher simply because of the comparatively short period-
during which they occur. Almost without exception they
breed among the wild forests and swamps to the north, so
perhaps their ability to evoke these places has something to
do with their special place in the bird-watcher's calendar. In
spring the passage is short and swift, but birds are often in
breeding plumage and a fine sight as a result. The last two
weeks of May and the first week of June are the peak period
for these birds. Bar-tailed godwits and knot in their 'reds' of

summer, sanderling brown instead of grey, turnstones in the colourful motley, dunlin with full black bellies and the graceful black terns living up to their name, all pass through. Two or three weekends and they are all gone.

The autumn period lasts longer, but a majority of the birds are youngsters and the adults, which in many cases pass through later having moulted along the way, are seldom in their finery. Spotted redshanks, resplendent in their black nuptial plumage, are an exception. Adult birds of this species arrive back on our marshes before the end of July only a matter of a few weeks after the last birds passed through on their way north. It has been suggested that such early arrivals are birds that have failed to breed.

The actual timing of passage in these high Arctic waders is variable and the different species are represented by varying numbers too. Some years may be good for little stints, others for curlew sandpipers doubtless depending on their success in breeding. There is always a scattering of the commoner species throughout August and September, and often favoured marshes are alive with waders. Many stay around for several weeks and at least some species stop over through-out the autumn to moult before continuing their journey.

Other species have a more leisurely approach to their autumn migrations as well. Skuas may gather at favourite terneries to rob the birds returning with food for late hatched young. These pirates are also attendant on the flocks of terns that regularly gather at the rich feeding grounds provided by sewage outfalls and nuclear power stations. The famous 'Patch' at Dungeness Power Station attracts all the regular British terns as well as interesting gulls and black terns. The latter are frequently found inland as well and will stay off-passage at reservoirs for days or even weeks.

It is this lack of hurry on the part of the birds that really gives an opportunity for the bird-watching grapevine to go into operation. Telephones buzz with the exchange of information every Sunday evening and those who wish have

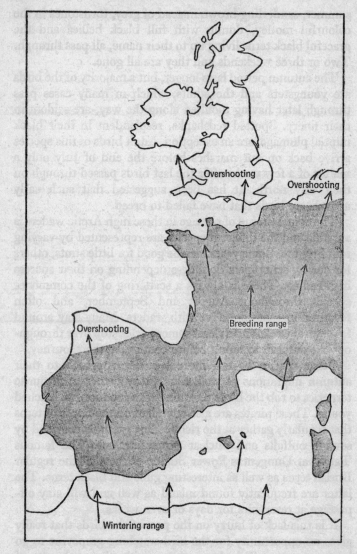

14. Migrating northwards in spring the hoopoe often over-shoots its breeding range to penetrate Britain and Northern Europe.

a real opportunity to set out and successfully see a particular bird.

Passerines are inevitably less confined than wetland birds. They may well stay off-passage for similar periods, but unless they have been located on a small and easy-to-work island they simply move away and become lost among the surrounding countryside. Yet in the same way as many passage migrant waders are scarce in spring and abundant in autumn, so too are bluethroats and barred warblers much more likely after, rather than before, the breeding season.

Not all birds are to be looked for in autumn. The phenomenon of 'over-shooting' regularly brings a number of birds to Britain in spring that usually nest well to the south. Most familiar of these is the hoopoe, a bird of May and June, but golden orioles, little egrets and a scattering of other southern species occur every year. Also to be included in this group is the red-footed falcon, small parties of which occur in one area near the south coast. These birds are virtually unknown in autumn.

## When to Watch Birds Abroad

To anyone unfamiliar with Britain and its birds I always recommend a visit in May or June. By this time all of the summer visitors have arrived, the resident birds are in the full swing of breeding, but there are still sufficient migrants passing through to change the birds to be seen on a daily walk. This is also the best time for the seabirds that act as a magnet to so many overseas bird-watchers.

It would be ideal to plan any bird-watching trip abroad to coincide with a similar happy situation, but unfortunately the passage of migrants and the local breeding season do not always coincide. In the Northern Hemisphere most birds breed between April and July; in the Southern Hemisphere between September and January. In the tropics many birds breed throughout the year while in other areas it is the end of the rainy season (not a phenomenon that we permanently rained-upon Britons find easy to comprehend) that sets birds breeding. The timing of migration, too, is highly variable, and it thus becomes quite impossible to summarise the best seasons for each and every part of the world.

It is, however, quite easy to find from the standard works of reference that cover an intended destination just when birds are breeding and whether or not such activity coincides with a migration period. For Europe the situation is quite straightforward.

Morocco and southern Iberia are best in April with visits to the deep south quite early in that month. France is a little earlier than Britain and May is altogether a fine month except in the mountains where a later departure in June is more productive. Over the whole of central Europe the breeding season is later than in the west and late May and June are very good. Denmark is similar to Britain, as is Holland and the north coastal region of Germany. Southern Scandinavia is good in June with hosts of Arctic birds passing through, though if you wish to catch the spectacular passage of cranes April is the month. This is also the best time to find those elusive Arctic owls, though earlier visits when the country is still in the grip of winter are even better for these birds. Northern Scandinavia is best visited in the second half of June, while in the extreme north, abutting the Arctic seas, early July is ideal.

The situation in the south-east of Europe is similar, though seasons tend to be slightly later. The Greek islands are good throughout April with breeding birds in profusion and good peaks of migration. Turkey too is good at this time though much of the high interior is still covered with snow and should be left until June. Yugoslavia is fine in early May, but further north the effects of a continental climate delay the start of the season considerably.

A successful bird-watching trip abroad is a result of careful preliminary work. The more time spent on planning the

better, when to go and where to go are the most essential
ingredients in such preparation and are well worth the efforts
made in research.

## A bird-watcher's diary

To plan a bird-watching year is sheer foolishness. We vary
in our approach to our hobby, to what we wish to see,
whether we are photographers or census workers and so on.
But presuming that you want to see as much of British bird
life as possible in twelve months, and that every aspect of
their lives is appealing, then certain opportunities must be
taken as they arise, or left for another year. While it would be
interesting to hear of anyone who followed the diary week by
week, its value will be as a prompter to those in search of an
idea of how best to spend a particular weekend.

I know of one American birder who swears that the best
place to live is in the heart of that continent and as near as
possible to an important airport. But even in tiny Britain
birds vary so enormously over the country that assumptions
about the ability to travel must be made. Here I assume that
the watcher is highly mobile, lives in southern England and
enjoys four weeks' holiday a year.

*January Week One:* an important week and one in which
New Year's resolutions are best kept. So we start off
trying to see plenty of new birds for the year by
visiting The Wash at Snettisham, Hunstanton and
Heacham. Book a permit for Minsmere for the third
week of April via the RSPB.

*January Week Two:* keep up the good work with a wild
goose chase around the Scottish Solway based at
Caerlaverock. Also visit Loch Ken, and the hills
beyond for possible golden eagle.

*January Week Three:* a trip round the London reservoirs
from Staines to Stoke Newington in an all out effort to
see the delightful smew, rare almost everywhere else.

*January Week Four:* Teesmouth for gulls. Among the many thousands of these birds present on the flats and the sea there may be a real rarity.

*February Week One:* spend the whole weekend and maybe a day of holiday as well as searching Lerwick Harbour for gulls and the adjacent voes for unusual sea duck and divers in Shetland.

*February Week Two:* enjoy a splendid day watching Bewick's swans, hordes of duck and wintering waders at the Ouse Washes, now virtually a continuous series of bird reserves.

*February Week Three:* pop down to Slimbridge to see most of the rest of the country's Bewick swans, the flocks of white-fronted geese and the incomparable wildfowl collection. Also make sure of a warm up in the tropical house with the hummingbirds.

*February Week Four:* once more we go to East Anglia, but this time in a search for crossbills which are well advanced in their breeding by now in the Brecks. Take the opportunity to have a look at some of the small local lakes for duck.

*March Week One:* Cley-next-the-Sea, the Mecca of British bird-watchers, to compare notes with everyone else and enjoy all of the wildfowl and other species the area has to offer. Check the great grey shrike on Salthouse Heath and the brent geese at Wells.

*March Week Two:* tour the Midland reservoirs – Eyebrook, Pitsford, Blithfield and then down to Grafham. Mainly duck, but chances of swans and other odds and ends.

*March Week Three:* resist the temptation to chase the first summer visitors on the south coast and determinedly head for the geese at Southport and the sandbanks full of waders at Lytham and adjacent areas of the Lancashire coast.

*March Week Four:* Dungeness and Rye in hope of the

first wheatear and chiffchaff, plus some seabird movements. Bound to be something else around at this time.

*April Week One:* first foray into the Common Bird Census with a long walk back and forth through an area of farmland with copses and hedgerows near home.

*April Week Two:* spring migration really getting under way so off to one of the south coast bird resorts – but which? Decide on Portland and take in Radipole as well. If things are quiet try to track down Dartford warblers nearby.

*April Week Three:* it has to be Minsmere for all of the arriving birds of summer. See the 'Scrape' and tour the woods and heaths, but do remember to book a permit well in advance.

*April Week Four:* back to the south coast again, this time for the huge passage of seabirds and waders that passes by Beachy Head at this time. Good chance of interesting passerines at Whitebread Hollow.

*May Week One:* north to Perthshire where crossing the Forth Bridge takes one into a great country of hills, forests and streams for black and red grouse and capercaillie. Ensure a good look at Loch Leven and see the RSPB Reserve at Vane Farm.

*May Week Two:* must get to Stodmarsh while the Savi's warblers are still reeling and enjoy passage waders and garganey.

*May Week Three:* a good time to go west to the islands and stacks of Pembrokeshire for seabirds. A day on Skomer photographing auks and kittiwakes may be followed by a tour, though not a landing, around the gannetry of Grassholm.

*May Week Four:* take a week to enjoy the delights of Shetland. By now red-necked phalaropes have arrived and Hermaness is full of great skuas and other seabirds. Get to Fetlar for snowy owl and much else besides.

*June Week One:* just the time to visit Cley for local

specialities including ruff, bittern, bearded tit and possible rarities. Make sure you are on the East Bank on Saturday afternoon to talk to other bird-watchers and pick their brains.

*June Week Two :* back to Scotland for the Spey Valley and the pilgrimage up to the Cairngorm heights for those specialities ptarmigan and dotterel. Golden eagle and osprey should also be seen here. Loch Morlich is a fine base.

*June Week Three :* the trouble with June is to fit everything in. You must visit your Common Bird Census area, but it seems a pity not to get to Walberswick for the east coast marsh specialities.

*June Week Four :* down to the New Forest for buzzard and Dartford warbler, Montagu's harrier and possible hobby – perhaps something else of note. Good birdwatching covering a variety of breeding species.

*July Week One :* the National Trust for Scotland organises various excursions during the summer to offshore bird islands. Consult them in advance and plan a trip to St Kilda, the ultimate in a British bird-watcher's experience. Spectacular seabirds.

*July Week Two :* many birds are still in full swing of breeding and early July is the opportunity to see those missed during May and June. Minsmere is a really good place for picking up a large range of such birds and nearby Havergate can be enjoyable just watching avocets defend their chicks. You have, of course, booked well in advance.

*July Week Three :* by now it is getting too late for breeding birds and we have missed the Farnes at their best. But roseate terns can still be seen, frequently from the nearby mainland. Anglesey offers another opportunity to search out this elusive species.

*July Week Four :* Dungeness is the place to pick up the first flush of returning summer visitors, and from now onwards all eyes will turn towards the coast and migrants.

*August Week One:* Cley's East Bank is lined with watchers checking the movements of returning waders. A few minor rarities will be viewable and make a point of checking the pines at Holkham where passerines are often of considerable interest.

*August Week Two:* many observers cannot resist the temptation to visit the east coast at every opportunity during the autumn, but passage elsewhere can be exciting too and we choose Portland for passerines and Radipole for little gulls.

*August Week Three:* there are just too many birds about and Minsmere is the place to see the most. Waders are all over the pools and the Sluice bushes may produce a few migrant warblers.

*August Week Four:* one of the peaks of the year and a natural time to get to Cley.

*September Week One:* high interest in migrants continues, but for a change we head to the south-west to Porth-gawarra and Marazion Marsh. Also pop along to that exquisite little estuary, the Hayle, where photographs of waders are a good possibility and to St Ives Island to have a look at the sea. We shall be back here later.

*September Week Two:* one cannot let a year go by without seeing the beauty of the Emerald Isle. So off we go to Cork for American waders at Akeragh Lough and seabirds including the larger shearwaters off Cape Clear. If you had the time a week would not be wasted.

*September Week Three:* all this concentration in the south and east is inevitable for the bulk of passage migrants occurs in this area. But the time has come to go north to visit Fair Isle, that haven of rarities and their watchers. Take a week and guarantee yourself a 'life' bird. Again you must book well in advance, the observatory is very popular at this time.

*September Week Four :* frequently sees good migrations of seabirds in the North Sea and the Spurn Peninsula in Yorkshire is a fine place to observe them. Passerines are sure to be found among the dense bushes and if a fall occurs you could have a fabulous time.

*October Week One :* St Agnes in the Isles of Scilly is the place for American landbirds and possibly waders, but even eastern rarities occur here with remarkable regularity. If you have not booked a year in advance stay on St Mary's.

*October Week Two :* a pity you could not stay on St Agnes another week but it's the same area that beckons back again. Try the Hayle for waders, but also shelter behind the wall at St Ives Island and watch the storm-driven seabirds battle their way out of the bay.

*October Week Three :* just the time to get back to Cley, anything may turn up at this time and something of interest quite definitely will.

*October Week Four :* I always go to Walberswick at this time and see no reason to change the habits of a life-time. May get a fall of thrushes, but snow bunting and shorelark are virtually certain and hen harrier very likely.

*November Week One :* dash north in the hope that you are not too late for the masses of geese that are arriving along the east coast of Scotland. Loch Leven is the best place with thousands of pink-feet.

*November Week Two :* winter visitors are still pouring in, but your activities may well be more geared to the weather and the possibilities of a wreck of seabirds. Hilbre Island in the Dee is a fine spot for vast flocks of waders and bird photographers enjoy fine opportunities at high tide.

*November Week Three :* Sheppey provides the best bird-watching within easy reach of London and we dash off to see waders there and along the north Kent

coast at Halstow. Very good chance of rough-legged
buzzard.

*November Week Four :* what a good opportunity to see the
geese and waders at Wexford Slobs in Ireland. Wintering waders include a scattering of the unusual.

*December Week One :* westwards again, this time to the
Tamar for avocets and other good waders on the
surrounding small creeks.

*December Week Two :* Langstone Harbour and Farlington
Marsh can be good at any season. Perhaps the brent will
be back and there will be plenty of waders anyway.

*December Week Three :* Islay in the Inner Hebrides has a
fine population of barnacle geese and choughs that we
have managed to miss during the rest of the year.

*December Week Four :* Christmas at Cley – what more
could any bird-watcher desire?

So ends another great year. You are well over two hundred
species and must have met hundreds of other bird-watchers
along the way. They will have told you of birds and places
that cannot be mentioned in a book of this nature. Next year
you will be in a better position to plan your own 'Where to
Watch Birds'.

# CHAPTER FOUR

# Where to Watch Birds

The bird-watcher's diary which completed the previous chapter is, in part, a guide to time and in part to places. To those who require more details on where to go I can only recommend (immodestly) my own *Where to Watch Birds*. But there is a lot more to the 'where' aspect of bird-watching than just knowing the hot spots. The more you know and understand about birds, the more birds you will find and the more you will enjoy them.

Birds are animals adapted to a specific mode of living. Because they can fly and are highly mobile, we tend to think that they can go where they please. In fact they are creatures of habit and are restricted (like the rest of us) by the need for food and shelter. They have survived by adapting to particular foods, to particular nesting habits, by adopting distinctive migration patterns and so on. The result is that all birds are in some way confined to particular habitats and life zones. Some, like the starling, are highly adaptable, others like the Dartford warbler are restricted to a particularly narrow life zone. To get the most from your bird-watching it is as essential to know where the birds go, as to know where to go yourself.

## Birds and their Habitats

The most widely used classification of habitats is that prepared for the BTO by W. B. Yapp and published in 1955. In very precise terms he classifies all the different niches to be found in the British Isles and, while a fundamental understanding of these is necessary for serious ecological studies, a broad familiarity with the major habitat types is a prerequisite of all who are interested in birds and the countryside in general. The list that follows picks out these major types together with the dominant and more interesting birds to be found in each. Because of the mobility of birds there is inevitably some overlap of species, but that is one of the things that makes watching birds such an appealing pastime.

## Deciduous Woodland

At one time woodlands, consisting of oak, beech, ash, birch and other trees, covered the major part of lowland England, but agricultural activities have been destroying them from earliest historical times. Today's broad-leaved woods are a curious mixture of natural and planted trees and include many introduced exotics. The pedunculate oak woods of south-east England have a quite different character to the sessile oak woods of the Welsh hill slopes, and different birds as a result. The beech hangars of southern chalklands, beloved of wood warblers in summer and bramblings in winter, are progressively being felled. Alders, a winter haunt of siskin, are invariably associated with bogs, and being continually destroyed by drainage, while our population of elms is in process of felling due to Dutch Elm disease.

Typical deciduous woodland birds in order of abundance:

*Pedunculate oak woods:* chaffinch, willow warbler, robin, starling, wren, blackbird, blue tit, great tit, song thrush, mistle thrush, redstart, chiffchaff, blackcap, garden warbler.

*Sessile oak woods:* chaffinch, pied flycatcher, wood warbler, willow warbler, robin, wren, tree pipit, coal tit, redstart, great tit.

*Beech woods:* chaffinch, great tit, blackbird, wren, wood

pigeon, willow warbler, robin, blue tit, blackcap, chiffchaff.

*Birch woods:* chaffinch, willow warbler, tree pipit, robin, wren, crow, blue tit, wood warbler, wren, yellow-hammer.

(After W. B. Yapp, *Birds and Woods*, *OUP*)

## Coniferous Woodland

Pines and firs are native to the more northern parts of Britain, though most of the vast, and expanding, areas covered by coniferous plantations throughout the country are of introduced species. In particular there are huge areas of spruce, larch, sitka and others. Many bird-watchers regard these new plantations as lacking in birds, whereas in fact they hold far more species and larger numbers than the same area of land held prior to planting. In moorland areas thin populations of wheatear and grouse together with the occasional merlin give place to different avifaunas as the plantation grows in height and age. Whitethroat and tree pipit are present during the early stages, while tits become dominant later as scrub gives way to forest.

The old Scots pine forests of the Spey Valley are as near as it is possible to get to the original forests that once covered so much of Scotland. They have been progressively exploited in times of national emergency, but their characteristic bird fauna remains.

Typical coniferous woodland birds in order of abundance:

*Speyside Scots pine forests:* chaffinch, willow warbler, coal tit, tree pipit, redstart, meadow pipit, goldcrest, song thrush, cuckoo, crested tit, crossbill.

*Mature spruce forests:* goldcrest, chaffinch, robin, wren, coal tit, chiffchaff, willow warbler, song thrush, blackbird, wood pigeon.

*Young spruce plantations:* meadow pipit, skylark, tree

pipit, whinchat, willow warbler, linnet, robin, white-throat.

(After Yapp)

## Scrub

The term scrub covers a multitude of different landforms most of which are transitional. Thus a young conifer plantation is a scrub zone, but so too are freshly coppiced deciduous woodlands. The chalklands of England have been invaded by scrub since the rabbit was decimated by myxamatosis, and while the dominant scrub species never become trees they shelter oaks and beeches that will eventually reach a climax of succession.

Hawthorn, elder and hazel are typical shrubs that invade open areas to form scrub, and they are invariably accompanied by brambles and gorse. In the south larger areas of gorse are inhabited by the rare Dartford warbler, but scrub more typically holds:

Whitethroat, lesser whitethroat, tree pipit, woodlark, nightjar, stonechat, whinchat, red-backed shrike, linnet, goldfinch as well as the more common species.

## Dry Field Vegetation

In this section field vegetation is used as a botanical term, i.e., the field layer, rather than in an agricultural sense. It refers to open areas where vegetation is dominated by low, ground cover. Thus most agricultural land does, in fact, fall into this category accounting for a large part of the land surface of this country. Root and cereal crops cover a large percentage of this area, though grazing remains an important section. The various sub-divisions of field vegetation are grassland, bracken, heath, moor and the alpine mountain tops. Grassland is incredibly variable from mown meadows to rough grazing, and heaths and moors split readily into a number of distinct types. They may consist of heather or ling, of cotton grass or bilberry. The birds of each type of field covering will similarly vary as they will according to height and latitude.

Typical open area birds:

*Grassland:* wheatear, corn bunting, skylark, partridge, lapwing, stone curlew.

*Grass Moorland:* meadow pipit, skylark, wheatear, twite, ring ouzel, merlin, lapwing, golden plover, dunlin.

*Bracken:* linnet, whitethroat, whinchat, woodlark, nightjar.

*Heath:* meadow pipit, wheatear, red grouse, skylark, dunlin, golden plover.

*Alpine:* meadow pipit, dunlin, golden plover, dotterel, ptarmigan, snow bunting.

## Damp Field Vegetation

Bogs have a characteristic flora all of their own but vary little in the way of bird life. The soil is acid and peaty and, while bog myrtle, sphagnum, ling and purple moor grass are dominant, the birds that can find a living in such conditions are few. Meadow pipits are ubiquitous, but other species use the difficult terrain to provide safe breeding quarters, while fighting to feed elsewhere. Thus some large gulleries are to be found on the high level bogs of the Pennines, while further north they are the resort of greenshank, dunlin and curlew.

## Marshes

Fresh marshes, in the sense used here, are vegetation-covered wetlands. Sometimes they are completely overgrown, but more often they abutt areas of open water. They thus shelter many birds that find a home in open waters (classified below as a distinct habitat). Thus birds such as ducks and grebes regularly nest among marsh vegetation, though frequenting open water to feed. Vegetation varies from sedge through reeds to water lilies. Typical species would be:

Sedge, reed and grasshopper warblers, great crested grebe, marsh harrier, bittern, bearded tit, gadwall, mallard, teal, moorhen, coot, water rail.

Several of these species are confined by factors other than pure habitat to areas of East Anglia where large reed beds provide them with a home.

## Inland Cliffs and Banks

The major difference between inland cliffs and sea cliffs is (tautologically) the absence of the sea from the former. Thus while most birds that breed on inland cliffs also breed on seacliffs, the reverse is not true.

*Rocky Inland cliffs:* jackdaw, crow, peregrine, golden eagle, kestrel.
*Sandy Inland cliffs:* sand martin.

## Open Fresh Water

Fresh water varies from the smallest village pond to the largest of lakes and includes high level tarns, meres and pools. Both size and depth are important characteristics in determining the variety and number of birds, for it is food and security that attract birds to open water. Only the grebes nest on the water, but even they anchor their floating nests to some emergent or overhanging vegetation. Others nest very close to open fresh water like the divers, while duck, geese and gulls find in the larger waters a secure roost.

A particularly valuable form of open fresh water from an

ornithological viewpoint is flooded grassland. Low-lying meadows which are flooded regularly every winter form superb feeding grounds for wildfowl and waders. They dry out during spring and are then the only home in Britain for black-tailed godwit with ruff, snipe, redshank, yellow wagtail and other species breeding as well.

Subsidence due to mining operations also creates permanent areas of shallow fresh water and as a result some of the best bird-watching to be found in mining areas.

Great crested grebe, little grebe, red-throated and black-throated divers, osprey, mallard, pintail, gadwall, shoveler, teal, garganey, tufted duck, pochard, coot, moorhen.

## Flowing Fresh Water

Though rich in food, flowing water does not hold anywhere near the number of birds as open still water. Nevertheless it is an important habitat for bird-watchers to explore. Moorhen, kingfisher, dipper, grey and pied wagtail and common sandpiper breed, and in winter green sandpipers are frequent visitors.

## Estuaries and other Inter-tidal Zones

Estuaries are the most productive landforms on earth. Every day they are covered and uncovered by the sea and among the mud and sand live teeming masses of molluscs and crustaceans. The biomass produced is more than that produced by a field of wheat, though man has not yet discovered a means of exploiting this richness. Not surprisingly, then, animals that have adapted to this habitat are particularly abundant and none more so than waders. Vast hordes of these birds use the feeding grounds all the year round reaching a peak in late autumn. Duck too find them rich feeding grounds and shelduck are particularly numerous. Cormorants, swans, spoonbills, ospreys, divers and grebes all utilise estuaries in their different ways.

Divers, great crested grebe, little grebe, whooper swan, mute swan, pochard, tufted duck, wigeon, teal, pintail, osprey, redshank, knot, dunlin, curlew, turnstone, grey plover, oystercatcher, lapwing, godwits, ringed plover.

## Coasts

The coastline of Britain is exceedingly varied and each type of coast has its own bird fauna. Sheer rocky cliffs boast a wealth of breeding seabirds that includes auks, gulls, shags, gannets as well as several land birds like jackdaws and peregrines. A seabird cliff is a sort of tenement within which each species occupies its own distinct niche. On the cliff tops puffins excavate their burrows, below on ledges guillemots stand in long rows. All around them fulmars occupy the deeper clefts while kittiwakes build an elaborate nest on the tiniest of ledges. Lower down razorbills hide deep among the rocks, while black guillemots can be found among the tangle of boulders at the edge of the sea. The largest shageries are among coarse screes.

Sand and clay cliffs are usually too low for all but a few gulls and fulmars, but may be ideal for sand martins. Dune coastlines are usually very much disturbed, but in more remote areas may hold colonies of terns and eiders. Shingle beaches support ringed plover, oystercatcher and little tern, while mud-lined shores and saltings are associated with estuaries and the birds that they shelter. In winter divers, grebes and sea duck occur, and rocky shores are frequented by purple sandpiper and rock pipit.

Divers, grebes, fulmar, gannet, shag, cormorant, scaup, wigeon, scoter, velvet scoter, peregrine, kestrel, estuary waders, purple sandpiper, turnstone, terns, gulls, auks, rock dove, jackdaw, chough, rock pipit.

## Seas

Most seabirds are coastal rather than truly pelagic. British breeding birds that are properly birds of the ocean include the small petrels, Manx shearwater, fulmar and kittiwake. Several other species are regular visitors to our seas mostly in autumn, and the great shearwater comes to us from remote Tristan da Cunha, a speck in the South Atlantic. Watching pelagic birds, other than at their breeding grounds, poses problems, for they usually remain out of sight of land. Promontories sometimes lie across their paths and during misty weather they may come quite close. In the United States birders charter boats specifically to seek out 'pelagics' and I am surprised that so few British watchers have followed suit.

Fulmar, Manx shearwater, Balearic shearwater, Cory's shearwater, great shearwater, Leach's petrel, storm petrel, kittiwake, Sabine's gull.

## Farms

Most of our land is cultivated or exploited by farmers in one way or another, and recent changes in agricultural techniques have had a considerable effect on the landscape and on the lives of all of the animals, including birds, that live there. Pesticides and herbicides have proved a disaster to many forms of life, and perhaps in the long run to ourselves. Crops with shorter growing periods allow less time for birds to breed successfully among them. Approaching half a million young deer are killed annually in Germany by farm machinery, so goodness knows how many eggs and chicks are destroyed.

Pasture and marginal land are being ploughed and hedges and dells are being rooted up and destroyed. The disappearance of hedgerows is a considerable tragedy, for they provide nesting and roosting sites for a wide variety of species. The result may create better conditions for the use of machinery, but there are dangers of soil erosion of which farmers are only too well aware.

As crops and land use are changed so too are the birds that live among them. Are there fewer hop yards and orchards? Are intensive market gardens increasing? Are old barns that provide a home for owls and swallows being replaced by modern structures devoid of nest sites? Are we not becoming too 'tidy-conscious' and reducing the variety of opportunities for birds to live on farmland?

Kestrel, lapwing, barn owl, skylark, corn bunting, yellowhammer, blackbird, song thrush, whitethroat, swallow, house martin, chaffinch, linnet, goldfinch, carrion crow, rook, magpie.

## Towns and Cities

Though generally poor in species, the density of birds in suburban gardens is the highest of any habitat in the country. By planting a variety of sheltering shrubs, by keeping grass cut and by active feeding and encouragement several birds have found gardens an ideal habitat. Tits, thrushes, blackbirds, spotted flycatchers all occur in great numbers. House martins and swifts are so dependent on our homes that it is a surprise to find these birds nesting in natural sites. Even city centres are not without their birds, and while parks really are just large gardens, the totally built-up area may shelter kestrels and jackdaws as well as house sparrows and feral pigeons. Following the last war black redstarts moved into the London bomb sites. Now that these have disappeared they are using redevelopment sites, power stations and factories instead.

Our urban needs for fresh water and sewage and rubbish disposal provide opportunities for a larger range of species to move in with man and take advantage of his artifacts. For the city dweller no better bird-watching can be found than on reservoirs, rubbish tips and sewage farms.

Kestrel, wintering duck, passage waders and terns, tawny owl, tits, thrushes, spotted flycatcher, house martin, swift, jackdaw.

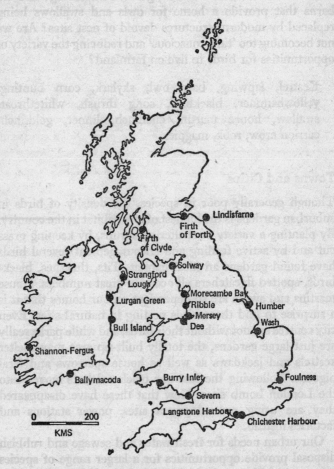

15. Britain and Ireland's top twenty estuaries.

## Top Spots: Estuaries

Wetlands, especially coastal ones, have always attracted birds
and bird-watchers. We are fortunate in this country in having
some of the world's finest estuaries, areas that are alive with
birds the year round. Here is a list of the best estuaries based
on wader counts undertaken by the BTO during the winter of
1972–3. Figures for each locality are total waders counted at
one time.

### Top Twenty Estuaries 1972–3

| | |
|---|---:|
| Morecambe Bay | 232,661 |
| Wash | 165,311 |
| Ribble | 158,581 |
| Dee | 154,140 |
| Solway | 144,191 |
| Severn | 75,924 |
| Firth of Forth | 62,526 |
| Shannon-Fergus (Clare, Limerick, Kerry) | 55,949 |
| Chichester Harbour | 44,887 |
| Foulness | 44,423 |
| Lindisfarne | 38,849 |
| Langstone Harbour | 38,329 |
| Humber | 37,586 |
| Lurgan Green (Louth) | 37,002 |
| Burry Inlet | 34,720 |
| Bull Island (Dublin) | 29,952 |
| Strangford Lough (Down) | 29,883 |
| Ballymacoda (Cork) | 29,632 |
| Mersey | 29,276 |
| Firth of Clyde | 28,432 |

(After Prater, 'Estuary Bird Survey', *BTO News*)

## Top Spots: Reservoirs

Few other published lists indicate so clearly where birds can be found, but a list of the best reservoirs for duck was published in 1963. Figures show total winter duck population, though not the importance for particular species.

*Top Fifteen Reservoirs in England and Wales*

| | |
|---|---|
| Abberton (Essex) | 8,370 |
| Chew (Somerset) | 3,445 |
| Blithfield (Staffs) | 3,295 |
| Pitsford (Northants) | 3,165 |
| Hollowell (Northants) | 2,190 |
| Hanningfield (Essex) | 1,855 |
| Blagdon (Somerset) | 1,725 |
| Eye Brook (Leics) | 1,880 |
| Staines (Middx) | 1,250 |
| Barn Elms (London) | 1,260 |
| Cropston (Leics) | 1,195 |
| Durleigh (Somerset) | 835 |
| King George VI (Middx) | 1,050 |
| Cheddar (Somerset) | 985 |
| Queen Mary (Middx) | 880 |

(After G. R. Atkinson-Willes, *Wildfowl in Britain*)

Since this list was published many new reservoirs have been constructed and some perhaps deserve a place here. Grafham Water (Hunts) covers 1,500 acres, is a noted haunt of duck and a good place for migrant terns and waders. The soon-to-be-opened Datchet Reservoir beside the M4 east of London Airport will doubtless become another fine spot in an already well established wetland complex.

In general lowland reservoirs are more productive than high level waters, but some Scottish hill reservoirs are regularly used as roosts by large numbers of geese.

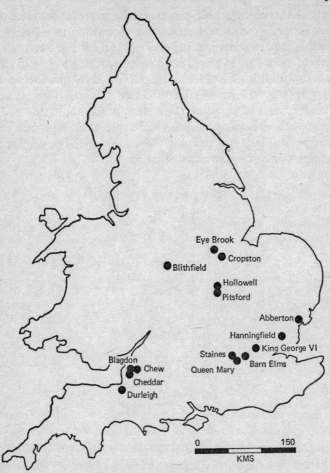

16. England's top fifteen reservoirs.

## Top Spots: Observatories

A network of bird observatories rings the coasts of Britain and Ireland. They are unofficial bodies established and maintained by enthusiasts, and while some are well established and virtually permanent, others come and go with the enthusiasm of the people concerned. Representatives meet to discuss policy and exchange ideas from time to time, but each is jealous of its independence. Most offer accommodation of some sort to keen bird-watchers willing to join in the work of finding and counting migrants and the routine work of trapping and ringing birds. They vary considerably in standard and while some offer clean and comfortable bedrooms others have dormitories more specifically designed for the young and the tolerant. Many are self-catering and bring-your-own-food establishments.

### BIRD OBSERVATORIES

1. Fair Isle
2. Isle of May
3. Spurn
4. Gibraltar Point
5. Holme
6. Sandwich Bay
7. Dungeness
8. Portland
9. Lundy
10. Skokholm
11. Bardsey
12. Walney
13. Calf of Man
14. Copeland
15. Cape Clear

Further details and addresses of these observatories can be found in *Where to Watch Birds*, or obtained from the BTO, Beech Grove, Tring, Herts.

### Top Spots: Rarities

Some areas are noted for the number of rarities that they produce. This in turn attracts bird-watchers who in their

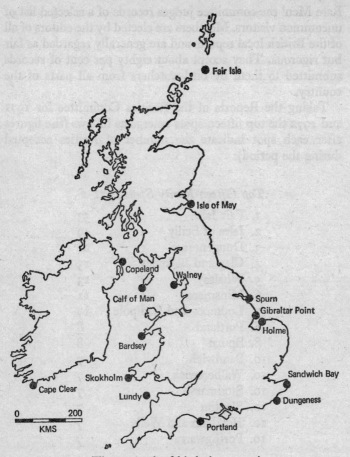

17. The network of bird observatories.

turn find even more rarities. Certainly once an area gets a name for attracting vagrants it is difficult to see it ever throwing it off.

The acceptance of reports of rare birds in Britain (excluding Ireland) is the function of the Rarities Committee of *British Birds* journal. Known affectionately as 'The Ten

Rare Men' the committee judges records of a selected list of uncommon visitors. Members are elected by the editors of all of the British local reports and are generally regarded as fair but rigorous. They accept about eighty per cent of records submitted to them by bird-watchers from all parts of the country.

Taking the Reports of the Rarities Committee for 1971 and 1972 the top fifteen spots emerge as follows (the figures after each spot indicate the number of rarities accepted during the period):

### Top Fifteen Rarity Spots 1971–2

|     |                      |    |
| --- | -------------------- | -- |
| 1.  | Fair Isle            | 53 |
| 2.  | Isles of Scilly      | 49 |
| 3.  | Dungeness            | 21 |
| 4.  | Cley and Blakeney    | 15 |
| 5.  | Whalsay              | 13 |
| 6.  | Minsmere             | 11 |
| 7.  | Lodmoor and Radipole | 10 |
| 8.  | Portland             | 8  |
| 8.  | Spurn                | 8  |
| 10. | Sandwich             | 7  |
| 10. | Walberswick          | 7  |
| 10. | Stodmarsh            | 7  |
| 10. | Slapton              | 7  |
| 10. | Holkham and Wells    | 7  |
| 10. | Porthgwarra          | 7  |

Two areas, at either end of the country, dominate the list. Fair Isle has an edge, but basically comes top because of its unique ability to attract certain species not normally found anywhere else. Scarlet rosefinches, in particular, are regular there in good numbers and give a boost to Fair Isle's total. The northern site also benefits from the regular trapping of birds that gives better opportunities for correct identifica-

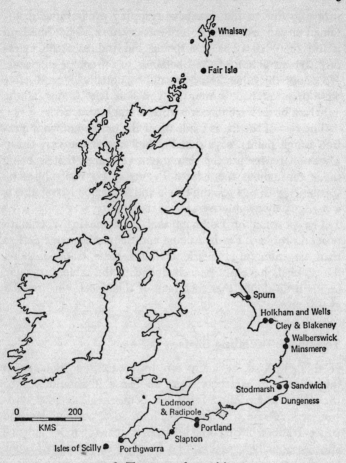

18. Top spots for rarities.

tion. The Scilly Isles cover a larger area and have a more general collection of rarities stemming from all points of the compass.

It comes as no surprise to find Dungeness and Cley high up on the list. Both areas swarm with watchers during the season, but here again the edge enjoyed by Dungeness is

probably due to the extensive trapping programme maintained at an established bird observatory. The Shetland
island of Whalsay is a surprise, but indicates the extraordinary attraction of the Shetlands to off-course migrants.
No doubt the other islands would be equally as productive
were they watched as intensively as Fair Isle. Almost all the
Whalsay birds were discovered by a single watcher.

The rest of the list is made up of the better-known migration watch points, save that Porthgwarra at the very tip of
Cornwall represents the new intensive search that is being
made throughout the Lizard Peninsula by rarity hunters.
Certainly with St Ives, the Hayle and Marazion Marsh this is
a particularly productive area of the country.

The position of Lodmoor and Radipole in Weymouth
poses a problem. For in August and September 1972 no less
than 22 immature aquatic warblers were trapped there.
These birds have not been included in the table, but there
seems little doubt that members of this species are regular
at this site.

## Top Spots: Breeding Birds

If the emphasis at many top bird-watching spots is on
migration and winter visitors *en masse* it should not be
thought that breeding birds are being neglected by bird-
watchers. Those who find migration so appealing also find
concentrations of breeding birds, as well as the more unusual
species, equally appealing. To travel to see birds is to look
for the unusual or the spectacular. For many species it is
unnecessary to travel very far. The Atlas Project of the BTO
has shown just how widespread are many species, some of
which we previously regarded as rather local in occurrence.
The finished Atlas will be a must for everyone interested in
birds and particularly to zoogeographers, ecologists and keen
bird-watchers. To give some idea of the widespread range
of our most common birds the table sets out the number of

10 km squares in which various species breed. The total is out of a possible 3,860 squares and the percentage figure can be regarded as the area of Britain and Ireland over which a species can be found.

### Top Twenty Most Widespread Birds

| | | | |
|---|---|---|---|
| 1. | Skylark | 3,775 | 97·8% |
| 2. | Carrion/hooded crow | 3,766 | 97·5% |
| 3. | Wren | 3,755 | 97·3% |
| 4. | Blackbird | 3,718 | 96·3% |
| 5. | Starling | 3,707 | 96·0% |
| 6. | Song thrush | 3,657 | 94·7% |
| 7. | Pied wagtail | 3,645 | 94·4% |
| 8. | House sparrow | 3,642 | 94·4% |
| 9. | Meadow pipit | 3,630 | 94·0% |
| 10. | Swallow | 3,592 | 93·1% |
| 11. | Robin | 3,590 | 93·0% |
| 12. | Dunnock | 3,574 | 92·6% |
| 13. | Chaffinch | 3,553 | 92·0% |
| 14. | Mallard | 3,548 | 91·9% |
| 15. | Kestrel | 3,540 | 91·7% |
| 16. | Willow warbler | 3,537 | 91·6% |
| 17. | Wood pigeon | 3,536 | 91·6% |
| 18. | Cuckoo | 3,526 | 91·3% |
| 19. | Blue tit | 3,473 | 90·0% |
| 20. | Reed bunting | 3,430 | 88·9% |

(After J. T. R. Sharrock, 'Atlas Project', *BTO News*)

It can be seen that the skylark, carrion/hooded crow and wren breed over 97 per cent of the surface of Britain and Ireland; and that the ubiquitous house sparrow covers no larger an area than the meadow pipit – usually considered a more geographically restricted species. It is also clear that few bird-watchers need to travel very far to see any of these birds.

In contrast, many consider seabird colonies well worth the trouble and effort needed to get to. Around our coasts and islands is one of the truly great sights in European ornithology. Though many colonies have been well known for centuries, no systematic investigation of all of the birds was undertaken until Operation Seafarer was organised by the

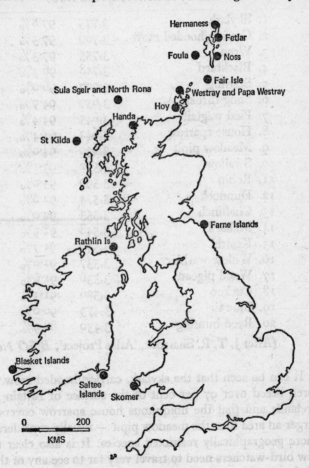

19. Top ten seabird colonies.

Seabird Group in 1969 and 1970. The results, published in the fine *Seabirds of Britain and Ireland* by Stanley Cramp, W. R. P. Bourne and David Saunders, have provided us with a staggering amount of data concerning the numbers of these possibly endangered birds. They also provide a guide to the major seabird stations together with their size and the number of species found breeding.

From the map it can be seen that major seabird sites are concentrated along our north and west coasts with pride of place going to Westray and Papa Westray in Orkney with nineteen species and a total population in excess of 100,000 breeding pairs. Other colonies of this order are found at St Kilda and Foula. Outside Scotland only five colonies can boast tallies of thirteen species, a figure beaten by no less

### *Top Ten Seabird Colonies*
*based on population and number of species*

| | | |
|---|---|---|
| 1. | Westray and Papa Westray | 19 species |
| 2. | Foula | 16 species |
| 3. | St Kilda | 15 species |
| 4. | Fetlar | 18 species |
| 5. | Noss | 16 species |
| 6. | Handa | 15 species |
| 6. | Hoy | 15 species |
| 8. | Sula Sgeir/North Rona | 14 species |
| 8. | Hermaness | 14 species |
| 10. | Fair Isle | 13 species |
| 10. | Farne Islands | 13 species |
| 10. | Skomer | 13 species |
| 10. | Blasket Islands | 13 species |
| 10. | Saltee Islands | 13 species |
| 10. | Rathlin Island | 13 species |

Map and table after S. Cramp *et al*, *Seabirds of Britain and Ireland* and reproduced by kind permission of the Seabird Group and Collins the publishers.

than nine Scottish colonies. The lesson for those who would watch or photograph seabirds is clear.

The rarer breeding birds pose a considerable problem for bird-watchers and writers alike. The whereabouts of many species are widely known, but seldom published. No doubt this is in part due to a conservatism on the part of protectionists, but the egg-collector is still a feature of the British bird scene and until he finally disappears we will have to pass information from one to another by word of mouth. The Savi's warblers at Stodmarsh in Kent were seen by hundreds of watchers long before their whereabouts were published and the area declared a nature reserve. Honey buzzards breed every year, but we must not say where. Marsh and Cetti's warblers, crested larks, bluethroats, serins, firecrests all remain cloaked in secrecy. Until they are safe and secure within reserves it must remain that way.

# CHAPTER FIVE

# Working for Birds

To become interested in birds is to care for their future. Yet, even in such an enlightened country as this, large numbers of birds are destroyed every year. Some are killed deliberately by shooting and traps, some are captured and imprisoned. Others are taken before they hatch from the egg. They are blown and their empty shells placed in the cabinets of oologists. Some are taken as chicks from their nest to be hand reared for showing among the cage bird fraternity, others to become the birds of falconers. Almost all such deliberate destruction of birds is illegal.

But for every bird deliberately killed many others die by accident as a result of human activities. The child that finds an 'abandoned' fledgling and takes it indoors for shelter kills it, despite his or her good intentions. When a fledgling leaves its nest, for a few days it cannot fly very well. While it is learning and gaining strength it is fed by its parents. When a fledgling is found its parents are nearby. Leave it and it will live, its parents are better able to look after it than you or I.

Our roads are dangerous enough to ourselves, but to birds they are lethal. Thousands are killed every year by cars and lorries, especially along narrow, hedge-lined lanes where it is difficult to see the approach of danger. Even town pigeons succumb every so often, and they are expert jay-walkers.

All of our activities affect birds in some way or another. Farming activities destroy nests and poison birds. We dump

waste in our rivers and in the sea. We spill oil and kill countless thousands of seabirds. We hit birds with our aeroplanes
and sometimes kill ourselves in the process. We disturb birds
simply by watching them, keeping them from their nests
and from feeding. But above all it is our effect on the landscape, destroying one habitat while creating another, that is
so important.

## Conservation

Every bird-watcher is a conservationist, even if only for the
selfish reason that he wants birds to survive so that he can
continue to enjoy himself. Most of us are conservationists
because we care for birds. But for the major dangers that
face birds we feel helpless. What can an individual do to
ensure that birds survive and prosper?

Clearly the first thing is to cease to be an individual and
become part of a larger group. By doing so your weight is
added to that of others who similarly care for birds and for
their future. You become part of a pressure group, and if the
group grows sufficiently large it will be able to influence
events through government and local authorities. In a
modern industrialised and competitive state, power is
everything.

The primary national body is the Royal Society for the
Protection of Birds, The Lodge, Sandy, Bedfordshire.
Within the last fifteen years the RSPB has grown from a small
club of some 10,000 bird-watchers to a national body of some
200,000 members. It has done so because more and more
people are concerning themselves with the environment in
which we live and which we share with birds.

The RSPB is no longer a bird protection society. It is a
progressive organisation with an ecological approach to
wildlife in general. Its reserves may be the centrepiece of its
operations, but it does much more besides. It spends
considerable amounts of money on education and publicity;

it produces its own films, arranges lectures and conferences and has established local groups that have taken over many of the functions once fulfilled, in part at least, by local naturalists' societies. No doubt the RSPB would dispute this but, in my view, it should be congratulated on setting up a grass-roots, but national, bird-watchers organisation. Within the RSPB bird-watchers can gain a great deal, but most of all it is the medium by which we can band together to speak with one voice to other groups within the country.

The government body concerned with conservation is the Nature Conservancy. The Conservancy has various obligations to protect wildlife and to encourage research. It maintains a string of establishments throughout the country, administers several hundred National Nature Reserves and is consulted on many aspects of planning. It is, nevertheless, a branch of the civil service with all of the disadvantages that that involves. The Nature Conservancy is particularly active in the field of research and notably poor at public relations. Visiting many National Nature Reserves is made intentionally difficult. Research comes first and naturalists usually require a permit and often a specific reason for requesting one. Hides and viewing facilities are poor or non-existent. No doubt a few reserves should be sacrosanct for the animals, plants and insects that live there. Others are properly out of bounds for research purposes. But, in general, I believe that the conservation movement needs to show people wildlife in order to grow and that National Nature Reserves should be open to visitors as freely as possible.

Though more specialised, the Wildfowl Trust is also a national body. The brainchild of Peter Scott, the Trust has its headquarters at Slimbridge in Gloucestershire where it maintains the largest collection of waterfowl in the world. It has its own research organization, is adept at public relations, earns much of its income from allowing the public to pass through the turnstile and view its wares, and is expanding its activities to other parts of the country. As the first 'bird garden' it has shown the way to the many who have followed it, but unlike other 'bird gardens' it devoted its income to thoroughly worthwhile activities. It saved the Hawaiian goose, the *néné*, from almost certain extinction and is active in protecting geese and swans, in particular, at its various reserves. Other conservation bodies could learn a lot from the Wildfowl Trust.

The Pheasant Trust works on similar lines and is concerned not with conserving the introduced pheasants that frequent our copses, but with conserving the world's pheasants on an international scale. Its headquarters at Great Witchingham in Norfolk house an excellent collection of pheasants and its activities are concentrated on breeding endangered species and reintroducing them to the wild. Perhaps we should have more such internationally minded bodies.

Below national level there are a whole host of organisations concerned with conservation. Many counties have county naturalists' trusts that own and/or administer reserves and negotiate with local authorities on matters of mutual concern. The trusts are not rich organisations, but can still achieve a great deal at local level by being aware of the possibilities of influencing companies and local authorities in respect of conservation. There are, for instance, a large number of freshly-created and flooded gravel pits scattered about the country that, at the end of their working life, have been converted to nature reserves. The full cost is borne by the company concerned, but this is invariably small and the company benefits from the good public relations value of being seen to care about the environment. Indeed, it has become a major feature of gravel company applications to develop a site, to stress the area will become a nature reserve once exhausted.

County trusts are also able to influence local authorities that, under the Town and Country Planning Acts, have powers to establish local nature reserves. It is a great pity that so few authorities have taken advantage of their powers under the provisions of these statutes. Some county trusts are continually pressing for them to do so and with considerable success.

## Bird-watching Organisations

Because of the cooperative nature of so much of the best ornithological work and of the quite natural interest of bird-watchers in each other, ornithological societies proliferate. There is hardly a corner of these islands that is not covered by a society, group or club, and many areas support several, sometimes competing, organisations. As well as joining one or more of these local clubs, most bird-watchers also join a national society to further their studies of birds.

In this respect pre-eminence must go to The British Trust for Ornithology, Beech Grove, Tring, Herts. The BTO consists of several thousand members, most of whom are active in some form of cooperative research. The Trust was created in the 1930s with the intention of drawing amateur researchers together to form a more productive unit and has eminently succeeded in its task. It organises the national Ringing Scheme, the Common Birds Census and the Atlas Project as well as many other shorter term inquiries. It holds an annual Bird-watchers' Conference and publishes *Bird Study* to record the activities of its members. Most bird-watchers with an interest that extends beyond feeding and ticking belong to the Trust.

The British Ornithologists' Union, c/o Royal Zoological Society, Regents Park, London, is the senior ornithological society and most established British ornithologists are members. The BOU's internationalism stems from more Imperial days, but the Union is being progressively modernised and up-dated. It holds meetings, conferences and supports research, but above all it produces, in *The Ibis*, one of the world's most important ornithological publications. Anyone with a serious interest in ornithology should join, but it is difficult to see what the average bird-watcher would gain from the Union, apart from the spuriously impressive letters MBOU after his name.

## Birds in Gardens

Feeding the birds is a pastime of considerable antiquity. But within the last fifty years, and especially since the war, it has become a small industry as well as a source of great pleasure to many. Every winter viewers are advised to feed the birds by television news commentators, and millions obey. Last winter I found it virtually impossible to buy those red-netted peanuts that tits and other species love so much. The shops had simply sold out.

Feeding birds can be an expensive business. A continual supply of peanuts and other seeds put out through the winter months can cost well over a pound a week. But the pleasure that so many people obtain from glancing out of their windows apparently makes such expenditure well worth while. Of course, it also benefits the birds.

Peanuts placed in hanging containers, nylon or metal, are the most universal bird feeders, but there are many others besides. Peanuts will attract blue, great, coal and marsh tits, greenfinches, the pesky sparrows and siskins. The discovery that red netfuls of peanuts attract the latter species is comparatively recent, but these birds are now regular feeders particularly towards the end of the winter when, perhaps, they have exhausted their more usual diet of alder seeds. Cheap spiral hanging feeders are not recommended. Experience has shown that it is easy for birds to catch a foot in them and then hang helplessly to die.

Many other species can be attracted by a bird table, for not all birds like to hang to feed. For preference a bird table should be covered with a roof, to protect food against the

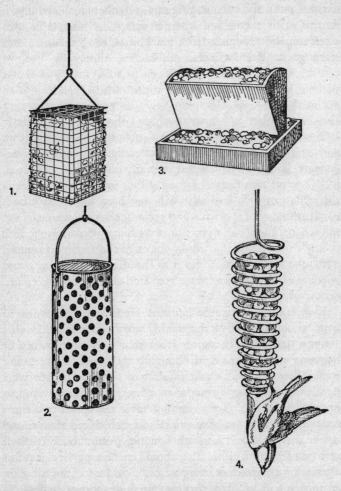

20. Bird-feeding furniture is varied to attract different species –
1. wire basket; 2. peanut cylinder; 3. wooden hob; 4. lethal spiral
peanut holder.

weather, and edged with a shallow rim to stop food falling to the ground and encouraging rats and other small mammals. Armed with seeds and kitchen scraps, a bird table will attract species ranging from blackbirds, song thrushes and starlings to woodpeckers, nuthatches, dunnocks and, of course, robins. Encouraging birds to feed with you is not without its risks. High concentrations of birds can lead to an outbreak of disease which not only infects the birds but may also be a threat to human health. Tuberculosis commonly infects the more gregarious birds including house sparrows and starlings. Salmonellosis, especially *Salmonella typhimurium*, is not only recorded in many outbreaks every year, but is a regular cause of food poisoning in man. A considerable proportion of outbreaks has been linked with high concentrations of sparrows and greenfinches attracted to food in gardens. Dead and dying birds are not a pleasant sight and, in any case, defeat the whole object of the feeding exercise. The disease is passed on via the birds' droppings and particularly by rats and mice attracted to food left overnight on the ground.

Lest too many would-be bird feeders are discouraged from what is basically a thoroughly worthwhile and enjoyable activity, it should be pointed out that only a minimum of hygienic precautions will eliminate the risks of spreading such diseases. Just as you would not serve a meal to your family on yesterday's unwashed plates, so should you clear up after the birds. Keep the bird table clean and free from decaying scraps that have not been eaten. Keep the ground below the table and beneath hanging peanut baskets clean and free from infection. You should make a particular point of moving the feeders every so often so that contamination of the soil is avoided. Accumulated droppings beneath a favoured perch are a potential source of bacteria and parasitic infection.

The avoidance of soil infection and the attraction of pests like rats and mice pose a problem because many birds prefer to feed on the ground and there has been a boom in encouraging reed buntings, fieldfares and redwings into gardens in recent years. Reed buntings are particularly fond of crushed oats, while windfall apples appeal to the migrant thrushes. Collecting windfalls in autumn and storing them until the hard weather of the new year is well worth while, though you will also find that starlings and blackbirds have a taste for your fruits. But do move the feeding site from time to time and only put out as much as the birds can eat during the day.

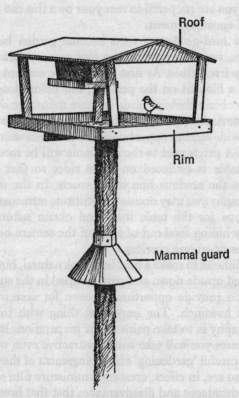

21. Bird table with essentials of design named.

Many species will come to water to drink and bathe and the provision of a bird-bath is a further encouragement to birds to seek out your company. Moving water is the only method that I know of that will attract summer warblers. A continual, but slow, drip syphoned from a large water container into your bird bath will bring in willow warblers, whitethroats and other somewhat shy birds. But you will have to be ever watchful to see them.

Mealworms, particularly in summer, delight many species and robins will quickly consume a plateful at a sitting. Unless you are prepared to rear your own this can be a costly form of encouragement.

Many bird-gardeners soon become garden bird photographers, for the opportunities that present themselves are virtually irresistible. At first you may be content to catch a shot of a blue tit on the peanuts, but before long you will want to obtain shots of birds in more natural positions. The simple device of placing an attractive perch next to the feeder will provide endless opportunities as the birds wait their turn to feed. A perch next to the bird table will be more effective if the table is enclosed on three sides so that the perch becomes the obvious line of approach. In the interests of photography you may decide to substitute attractive branches or stumps for the table itself and obtain natural looking shots by hiding food out of sight of the camera between the branches or among crevices.

It is difficult to make a bird bath look natural, but a dustbin lid placed upside down and partly buried in the surrounding earth can provide opportunities even for secretive species like the hawfinch. The important thing with this type of photography is to take pains about preparation. Ensure that the pictures you will take will be attractive even without the bird by careful 'gardening' and arrangement of the surroundings. You are, in effect, creating a miniature film set with all of the advantages and disadvantages that that involves.

Such 'controlled' conditions are also ideal to 'catch' birds in flight. You can focus your camera at a point between perch and feeder with some degree of certainty that a bird will eventually pass that way. With high speed electronic flash and an automatic triggering device flight shots can be obtained of a good variety of species. But now we leave the realm of bird-watching and enter the area of wildlife photography.

22. Even a dustbin lid can be made into a natural pool with a little care.

Encouraging birds into the garden is more than just offering them food and drink. You can provide them with homes in the form of nest boxes and nest sites. Hole nesting birds like the tits find nest boxes of the right dimensions and with a correctly sized hole virtually irresistible. But many other species can be persuaded to take advantage of your generosity if you provide the right type of nest box in the right position. An open-fronted nest box will be readily occupied by robins and spotted flycatchers, while a similarly designed, but much larger, box may well attract tawny owls and kestrels. A normal tit box filled with expanded polystyrene will suit the willow tit which nests naturally in a hole that it excavates itself in a rotting tree stump. The same box with a slightly larger entrance hole may suit a nuthatch which will promptly cement-up the hole to the correct size with mud. Trays placed on the beams of barns with a high

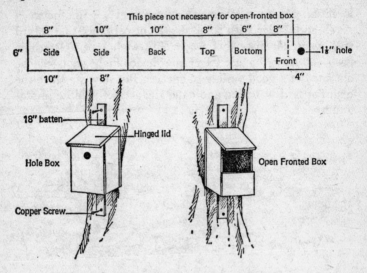

23. How to construct a nestbox.

entrance through a window, or hole in the brick-work, may attract a barn owl or a kestrel. In fact ingenuity is continually adding to the variety of species that can be persuaded to nest with us. A wooden barrel lodged in the crotch of a tree with half its end removed may suit a tawny owl or kestrel even in suburbia. Forty-gallon barrels are generally considered ideal, but sixteen-gallon ones also serve well enough.

All nest boxes have some things in common. They should be well made and well secured out of the prevailing wind and sheltered from the extreme heat of the sun. Over most of Britain this means placing them on the east or north-east of the tree or building. The walls of the box should extend to include the base, and the roof should be sloping to enable water to run off. After that it matters not at all whether boxes are constructed of rough, bark-covered boards, or planed wood, just so long as the inside is rough enough to allow the chicks to grip the wood in their climb to the exit. Birds do not need a perch near the entrance, but will use it if there is one. Boxes may be fixed against a tree, a shed, or against the wall of a house. In Holland nest boxes for kestrels have been placed atop poles in completely treeless areas and still the birds have taken to them.

But nest boxes are not the end of encouraging birds to breed. A band of bark nailed to a tree will suit a treecreeper. While a year ago I encouraged a pair of swallows to nest with us by erecting a suitable ledge on which to build their nest in an outhouse. A pile of brushwood piled against a tree will suit blackbirds and song thrushes and they may use the newly-created 'bush' over and over again.

The range of opportunities open to the bird-gardener is infinite. He may provide food, water, nest boxes and sites, and still seek for more. Planting trees and shrubs specifically for birds is a long term labour-saving investment. Most berry-bearing shrubs are good for birds but cotoneaster, with its plentiful supply of berries, is particularly likely to attract them. Hawthorn and birch are good for birds providing both food and shelter, while the bird-garden without an evergreen loses the opportunity of sheltering birds, particularly at night in winter when dense bushes provide both warmth and safety.

Unfortunately, although birds will attack the vegetable patch it is natural regeneration, when the land is colonised by nettles, by hogweed and other 'weeds', that birds find most attractive. Weeds not only provide seeds for birds in autumn, in summer they are a home to the countless insects on which most birds rear their young. A garden full of flowers and weeds (rather than lawns) is ideal for insects and, therefore, for birds. The tidy gardener who wages a battle against weeds and removes dead and dying trees will not make a bird-gardener, but he still may get a great deal of pleasure from those birds that can tolerate his activities.

## Top Bird Food Plants

| Plant | No. of Bird Species |
|---|---|
| Elder | 32 |
| Hawthorn | 23 |
| Yew | 17 |
| Blackberry | 17 |
| Cotoneaster *C. simonsii* | 12 |
| Rowan | 12 |
| Cotoneaster *C. horizontalis* | 11 |
| Barberry | 9 |
| Firethorn | 6 |
| Cotoneaster *C. watereri* | 5 |
| Holly | 5 |
| Crab Apple | 5 |

(After P. J. Olney, 'Birds and Berries'; *Birds*)

The bird-gardener concerned with attracting the largest
variety of species should clearly plant plenty of elders,
hawthorns and blackberries. Yew trees, poisonous to man
and animals, nevertheless provide food for birds without
any apparent harmful effects. But these are plants upon
which birds feed directly; many others such as birches and
willows not only provide seeds in autumn but shelter a
variety of insects in spring and summer. Perhaps no tree is as
bountiful in this respect than an old mature oak, but the
bird-gardener who plants an acorn is clearly thinking in the
long term, for these trees are very slow to grow and mature.
Flowers in profusion attract insects, and they in turn
attract birds. Though few will want a garden full of brambles,
nettles, dandelions and thistles at least a small corner may be
devoted to these fruitful species.

Setting up nest boxes and feeders, and bird-gardening in
general, places an obligation on the individual responsible.
By encouraging birds we become, in part at least, liable for
their safety. To set up a bird table that can be reached by the

neighbour's cat may be a disaster. To encourage birds to nest where people may easily see the nest box is sheer stupidity. To put food out every day and then go away for a Christmas holiday, without making arrangements for someone else to carry on the good work, is virtually criminal. When you take on a bird garden you take on a responsibility – do not forget it.

## Bird Reserves

The former owner of Brownsea Island in Poole Harbour kept it as a strictly private bird reserve where nature could take its course. As a result its appeal to birds gradually diminished and when she died it was an overgrown jungle that supported no more species than a neglected woodland on the nearby mainland. Thus we see the paradox of nature conservation. Left to its own devices much of our country-side would quickly revert to a scrub of birch and willow which, in turn, would gradually be replaced by forests of oak and beech. When myxomatosis struck down the rabbit population of England, areas of grassy downland were quickly invaded by thorn and within a few years grassland had turned to thicket. Letting nature take its course is natural, but it does not make a nature reserve.

Nature is dynamic, not static and in balance, as we were told at school. Left to its own devices it would work to a climax. As an area changes so too do the birds that inhabit it. An area of moorland may support a few meadow pipits, ring ouzels, wheatears and merlins. Planted with conifers it soon becomes alive with grasshopper warblers and whitethroats. As the conifers begin to dominate the landscape all of these disappear to be replaced by great tits and goldcrests. As conservationists we have a choice of which birds we want to live on our reserves. In some cases we decide that we would like as many species as possible and so we start to control nature so that as wide a variety of habitats as possible is available for birds. In other cases we decide that we wish to encourage those species that are having a tough time, those that live in habitats that are fast disappearing. Of course if you can begin with an area that is more or less what you want, you start with immense advantages. But even if the newly-acquired reserve is poor (like Brownsea Island), as long as the potentiality is there it can be transformed into what is required.

One of the best examples of this new dynamic approach to bird habitats is to be found at the RSPB's Minsmere Reserve in Suffolk. Here, with the help of the Army and its bull-dozers, a series of shallow coastal lagoons have been extended to create 'The Scrape', an artificial bird breeding and feeding site of immense importance. The lagoons existed before the Army moved in, and sheltered a few passage waders: the rest is artificial. Islands covered with polythene (to prevent weeds choking them) have been created and the sheeting covered with pebbles. Here the little tern has at last been persuaded away from the beach with its bathers and holiday makers. Avocets breed alongside common and Sandwich terns.

These habitat-creating activities are dramatic, but throughout the country control of habitat, clearing thickets and overgrown pools, controlling water levels to preserve unique reed beds, constructing artificial breeding sites, felling, blowing up as well as planting trees are part of what nature reserve maintenance is all about.

No better example of this dynamic and creative approach to reserves can be found than the creation of a gravel pit nature reserve at Sevenoaks by Jeffery Harrison and his helpers under the aegis of WAGBI and the Wildfowl Trust. Here the exhausted parts of a gravel pit have been planted and landscaped to provide optimum conditions for wildfowl. They are offered security, food, shelter and nest sites. As a result the winter population of wildfowl has increased enormously. But summer birds have benefited too and many interesting passerines now breed. Even rare migrants pop in, but that is probably more a result of Dr Harrison's en-thusiastic watching than of any 'extra' ingredient in his creative endeavours.

# CHAPTER SIX

# Studying Birds

At first we are content to identify the birds we see, to watch and enjoy them and become familiar with their everyday lives. Gradually we seek to know more. We dip into books, subscribe to magazines and journals, attend lectures, join societies and clubs – but most of all we begin to watch birds in a different way. Our watching becomes purposeful. Of course, such watching needs a background in ornithology to understand what things to look for, but an intensive course of reading together with regular field trips in the company of other bird-watchers soon gets most of us going on research of some sort.

'Research' is a formidable word. It smacks of sterilised laboratories and has a musty, old book smell to it. In many areas of knowledge, such as physics and chemistry, research is the preserve of white-coated PhD's backed by the resources of universities or international companies. With birds it is different. Britain and Ireland have a long tradition of amateur ornithology and, in any case, birds lend themselves very easily to amateur research. If a bird-watcher wants to study some aspects of the lives of birds he can just go ahead and do so. Many of the most important aspects of birds' lives have been described by amateurs working on their own. A teacher called David Lack could not stop looking out of his classroom window to watch the colour-ringed robins that haunted the school grounds. The result was the classic *The Life of the Robin*, and David Lack became director of the Edward Grey Institute in Oxford. While there may now be

more professional ornithologists than in Lack's day, there
are still more birds than professionals to cover them. Thus
research in our field is full of possibilities for amateurs to
contribute in a positive and meaningful way.

Research may be individual or organised, and may consist
of field work or museum and library study. Some types of
research lend themselves to field work such as the study of
breeding behaviour, whereas others concerned, let us say,
with the distribution of a species are essentially researches
through published material. It is just not possible to learn
where a bird is found by searching for it, one must rely to a
large extent on the efforts of others. But this does not make
such research unproductive. There are untold amounts of
information buried in miscellaneous journals which could be
collated and published, but ornithologists seldom seem to
have the time or money to do so. John Parslow's work on the
distribution of British birds is a case in point. Almost all the
information on which his important series of papers was
based was taken from county bird reports, hundreds of them.
The result was a fine series of accounts and maps showing
where birds are found throughout the country.

## Ethology

Ethology, the study of animal behaviour, is often thought of
as the preserve of the psychologist. It is not. Bird behaviour
can be watched and noted by anyone with an eye to see.
Edmund Selous, a keen bird-watcher, produced some of the
most important bird books published this century, sum-
marising his observations of many common European
species. Anyone who would follow in his steps should read
his books. Indeed to study bird behaviour it is necessary to
read what others have achieved before you, if you want to do
anything of any significance. But it most definitely is not
necessary to have reached degree standard.

If bird behaviour interests you, study it. Watch carefully

and record exactly what you see. What the subject and other creatures do, what their reactions are one to another. Omit nothing, for the very detail that you require may only be visible in retrospect. Try to record as much as possible, for too much data is certainly better than too little.

We hear a great deal about ornithological expeditions to remote and romantic sounding islands. For a long while this was my ideal – the desert island, myself and thousands upon thousands of birds. I wanted to conduct experiments, giving individual birds numbers, record the intimate secrets of their lives and spend happy hours logging all the data I collected by the light of a hurricane lamp under canvas and a clear, star-lit sky. Actually, I am sure that I would have whiled away my days happily watching and photographing birds and searching the island for migrants: until I became bored. It is not within all of us to undertake this sort of work and such expeditions are rightly the preserve of the accomplished, those who have shown that such work suits them, that they get results.

If your ideas of research seem to lead towards the desert island approach, forget it. Ethology benefits most from work on birds that are common and easy to watch near the observer's home. Indeed seabirds are the best subjects for case studies only because large numbers are concentrated in small, easy-to-work locations, and because they are generally easy to see and comparatively tame. The observer can watch a great many individuals in a very short space of time. So never try to study the behaviour of a rare or elusive species when a common and tame one would do just as well. There are still plenty of subjects within a mile of anyone in Britain.

If the study of bird behaviour is essentially an individual activity, inquiries into distribution are clearly cooperative affairs. Some years ago in London I organised a three-year survey into the breeding distribution of the house martin. On addressing the Annual General Meeting at the end of the second year I was delighted to be able to report a full one

hundred per cent increase in the number of observers. One
other observer had joined me in the search! Most small scale
surveys do little better. In contrast the BTO's Atlas Project
has been an enormous success.

Based on the National Grid 10 km squares, into which
Britain is divided, bird-watchers have volunteered to systematically search the square nearest their home for breeding
birds over a period of several years. The result has been
an incredible increase in our knowledge of birds in Britain.
It was the element of competition, with one's own record as
much as with others, perhaps, that made for such success.
There was always the chance of another bird, new for the
square, to be found in a seldom-visited part of the allotted
zone. As a result habitats were searched that had not been
visited by ornithologists before; for bird-watchers tend to
concentrate at those places that are acknowledged as productive. Spotted crakes, formerly considered a very rare and
irregular breeder, but one that is so easy to overlook, were
found here and there throughout southern England. Other
easy-to-miss species were found to be much more widespread than we had realised.

Operation Seafarer, organised by the Seabird Group, was
an attempt to count all British and Irish seabirds so as to
provide a base for monitoring the populations of these much
threatened species. Almost every mile of seashore was
covered and every cliff and stack examined. Some species,
because of the nature of their lives, proved impossible.
Others could be no more than sampled. But for a majority
of seabirds we now have a good idea how many there were
in 1970–2. This will now act as a yardstick against which to
measure changes in populations.

## Breeding Censuses

Population censuses last for a specific period and are then
complete. Doubtless they will be repeated from time to time,

perhaps every ten years or so. Other investigations are open-ended. One of the most important of these is the Common Bird Census of the BTO.

While it is possible (albeit difficult and time consuming) to count all the colonial seabirds, it is clearly beyond the scope of anyone to count many land-based birds. "How many willow warblers or blackbirds are there in the country?" is not a question to which anyone can expect an exact answer. Clearly there will be more at the end of the breeding season than at the beginning and that, incidentally, is why autumn is so much more fun for bird-watching than spring. If it has been a good breeding season there will be more birds than if the weather has been foul. Thus the only significant number from a population angle is the number of pairs that commence breeding. Imagine covering every square yard of Britain and Ireland counting breeding pairs of blackbirds.

Because of the use to which we wish to put any information gleaned on bird populations, there is actually no need to count all the birds. We want to keep an eye on populations so that if there is a sudden drop or boom we can note it quickly, investigate and perhaps do something about it.

The whole thing really started back in the 1950s when many watchers noted declines in the numbers of what were previously quite common birds. Gradually the decline began to be linked with the use of toxic chemicals used as insecticides and seed dressings (the chlorinated hydrocarbons). These persistent chemicals eventually found their way into the body tissue of birds of prey and there was a catastrophic decline in the number of peregrines. As a result effective preventive measures were taken just in time. It was nearly too late for the peregrine.

Frightened that they had not known about the affects of change on bird populations, and anxious that a similar disaster should be recognised earlier, the BTO introduced the Common Bird Census to monitor changes in the population of our commonplace birds.

Basically an area of some one hundred acres of farm or woodland is selected and visited by an observer five or more times during the peak of spring activity. On each visit the exact position of each singing male bird is plotted on a map. At the end of the season, when all the summer migrants, as well as the resident birds, have settled down to breeding, the maps for each visit are laid over one another and a single map drawn of the completed season's work. From this it is possible to see that the various individual birds have maintained their territories, for records of singing males in different months form clusters in the final map. These clusters are counted and the number of singing males of each species totalled up for the year.

While the Common Bird Census does not count every bird in Britain, it does give us an accurate idea of whether a

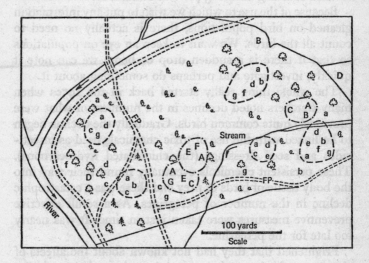

24. Common Bird Census of a plot of woodland showing territories of three pairs of robins (capital letters and – · – · –) and five pairs of willow warblers (small letters and – – –) plotted over seven visits (A – G).

particular species is doing well or not. CBC workers are scattered throughout the country covering every type of habitat. Some have been covering the same area for ten or more years and have enjoyed every moment of their constructive field work as well as the fascinating compilation of maps and drawing together of the final results.

When a picture for the whole country emerges we can see the remarkable recovery that birds can make after an exceptionally hard winter has decimated their numbers. When observatories report fewer whitethroats in spring, CBC workers can be asked to forward their results for the species as a matter of urgency. The usefulness of the CBC cannot be overrated, nor can the enjoyment that it creates.

The BTO are always interested in volunteers to take on new areas as CBC projects, but only from fully capable and experienced bird-watchers. So don't write to them within a month of buying your binoculars. See a couple of hundred British birds first.

## So you want to be a ringer?

The study of birds by individually marking them with rings is a comparatively recent one. Yet in the space of sixty years it has led to a complete revolution in our understanding of their lives. Migrant birds have been proved to fly vast distances to and from regular summer and winter homes and they even stop off at the same places along the way. Such facts are well known, and accepted as the major results of ringing, but we gain much other information besides. We know exactly how long an individual wild bird lives. We can calculate the population of a species by comparing the rate at which ringed birds are retrapped in a particular area with the chances of retrapping. We take advantage of handling a bird to measure it, note its state of moult and weigh it. If, as often happens, the same bird is retrapped in the same area the same measurements can tell us whether or not the bird is gaining weight and how far it has progressed with its moult in a specific period of time. We can find out how old a bird is when it first starts to breed and much more besides.

Taking wild birds for ringing requires a licence from the government, and almost all ringers meet the stringent qualifications required, by holding a permit from the BTO which organises the national ringing scheme. To obtain a permit is a long and painstaking job. Would-be ringers must be trained by existing ringers and serve a sort of apprenticeship. They must learn how to catch birds safely, how to handle them, how to put rings on and keep accurate records. They must learn the rules and regulations concerning what birds they may or may not ring. So the starting point is to contact a local ringer (address from the BTO, minimum age sixteen years) or visit a bird observatory.

Today most birds are caught in mist nets, fine black terylene nets that disappear when hung against a dark background. These nets must be carefully sited (they can catch cows and people too) and visited every fifteen minutes or so. Birds fly into a mist net and drop into a pocket of netting below a shelf string. There the majority lie still until they are extracted by the ringer – not a job for the clumsy or quick-tempered. Some species, notably blue tits and starlings, fight furiously to escape, grabbing footfuls of netting from all directions. The longer they are left the longer they take to extract. Sometimes a blue tit will tie itself in a virtual ball of netting and pose a considerable problem for the ringer. In extreme cases the ringer must be prepared to cut his net to extricate a bird safely.

A trapped bird is marked with a light alloy band placed around the tarsus. This is stamped with a serial number and the words 'INFORM BRITISH MUSEUM (NAT. HIST.) LONDON S.W.7' which is the clearing address for the British ringing scheme. Reports on and rings recovered from dead birds should be sent to The Ringing Officer, BTO, Beech Grove, Tring, Herts. In return the finder receives details of where the bird was ringed and the distance it has travelled to reach him.

Despite expressed fears, ringing, when carried out by an expert, does no harm to the bird. If it did the whole point of it would be destroyed, for the aim of ringing is to study the normal behaviour of normal birds. Accidents do happen, but they are very few indeed, and the gains in knowledge far outweigh the tiny element of risk. Even the RSPB now allows

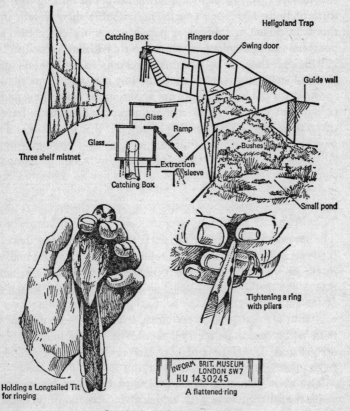

Heligoland Trap

Catching Box

Ringers door

Swing door

Guide wall

Glass

Ramp

Glass

Bushes

Three shelf mistnet

Extraction sleeve

Catching Box

Small pond

Holding a Longtailed Tit for ringing

Tightening a ring with pliers

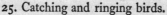

INFORM BRIT. MUSEUM
LONDON SW7
HU 1430245

A flattened ring

25. Catching and ringing birds.

some ringing to be carried out on its reserves for specific projects. It wanted to know, for example, whether the avocets, which the Society so lavishly protects in Suffolk, were the same birds that wintered on the Tamar Estuary in Cornwall. Only ringing could provide the answer.

At one time ringers simply ringed; but now they take full advantage of their opportunities to extract the maximum amount of data from the living bird in the hand. Weighing is particularly important. During the day a bird's weight varies considerably, but prior to migrating birds put on fuel in the form of body fat. Some species may double their weight in this way. From weights it is possible to work out a bird's potential range, that is how far it can fly without 'refuelling'.

Ringing, then, is a powerful weapon in the hands of ornithologists and conservationists, but it is also a fine field sport. With the happy decline of shooting for collections and oology (egg collecting) other more acceptable activities have taken their place. The hunting instinct, if that's what it is, is now channelled into tick-hunting, ringing and photography. All of which demand skill and craft in reaching a good standard.

## Counting Birds

The average bird-watcher's diary is full of figures. Figures of birds seen at certain places at certain times. While personally interesting, such figures are generally worthless. The fact that I saw a thousand black-tailed godwits on the estuary of the Suffolk Blyth in May is of no significance unless I can say, with some degree of certainty, that there were no more than a thousand. Better still would be to document their arrival and departure and correlate my figures with those from other estuaries up and down the East Anglian coast.

The channelling of this propensity to count birds into some useful form was first achieved by the monthly Duck Counts organised by the Wildfowl Trust. Every water of significance to ducks is counted by a team of observers during the middle of each month, usually the Sunday nearest the 15th. As a result we have built up an understanding of wildfowl movements, locations and the significance of particular waters. Some waters are so large that they have to be tackled by teams of observers, whereas others can be comfortably covered by an individual. Duck Counts are an immensely popular form of research, for many of the observers would be doing the same thing anyway without the advantage of feeling useful and part of a team.

Strangely enough it took a long time for these counts to become internationalised. So while a picture of the winter population of ducks, geese and swans was quickly established for Britain and Ireland, the exact significance of our populations of these birds in European terms could only be guessed at. The International Wildfowl Research Bureau (IWRB), with its headquarters at Slimbridge, home of the Wildfowl Trust in Gloucestershire, now ensures that coordinated censuses are taken throughout western Europe. This gives us a picture of the total population of the Atlantic flyway and the significance of Britain as a winter home for these birds.

In the last few years IWRB has extended its interests to other wetland species, particularly waders, and to other areas of the world. The Bureau has established specialist groups to coordinate work on geese, duck and waders. It has created regional committees to cover previously neglected and under-worked areas of the world like Africa and Asia. Such an international approach is to be encouraged, for once again those interested in wildfowl are showing the way to the rest of us. IWRB publishes a regular *Bulletin* on a yearly subscription basis which is packed full of international news, and is a good source of information on birds and bird locations otherwise unavailable.

The recent concentration on waders is due, in no small part, to the increasing development that threatens our estuaries. These exceedingly rich areas concentrate birds into countable areas, not only when they are feeding, but particularly when, driven off the mud flats, they concentrate at high tide roosts. With a variety of counting techniques the total population of wader species for the country can be ascertained with a remarkable degree of accuracy.

All of these cooperative ventures add purpose to our bird-watching. They require skilful identification and a certain experience of counting densely packed flocks of birds. Asking inexperienced observers to estimate even small flocks can produce startlingly different results. Following my experience as a teacher I always try to divide large flocks of birds up into 'classes' of thirty, and then see roughly how many 'classfuls' I can divide the flock into. Another useful technique is to count a part of the flock, say a hundred, and then estimate the number of hundreds. You will be surprised how small 'vast' flocks become with a technique of this sort.

## Other activities

The techniques of studying birds are numerous and varied. Museum workers produce important papers on birds without leaving the confines of their skin collection. Others may spend hours studying the migration of birds without taking their eyes from a radar screen. But for most bird-watchers it is contact with the wild and free living bird that they find so fascinating and research that takes us away from that has little appeal. Not for us the dusty museum and library, or the clean and clinical computer. We want to watch birds with a purpose.

For many the network of coastal observatories offers the ideal opportunity. We can see and record rare birds and still feel that we are adding to the accumulated fund of orni-thological knowledge. We may spend every weekend of the spring and autumn searching for migrants, ringing and weighing them or simply counting them. But there is much to be said for a daily dose of what does you good.

For several years I walked across my local open space in London every day of the year on my way to work. Throughout the spring and autumn I noted every migrant I saw in a daily log. When compared with arrivals of migrants at other inland observation points nearby, it was interesting to see that some large arrivals coincided and that others did not. Comparison with the records of the nearest coastal observatory at Dungeness showed a similarly interesting pattern of synchronisation, or the lack of it. Numbers were seldom large and twenty or so willow warblers sent me into deliriums of happiness. But the fact that migrants were present every day throughout the months of April, May, August and September, in a small and rather inhospitable area of urban London, was something of a revelation. From time to time surprise species like wood warbler, pied flycatcher in spring, cuckoo and others would drop in. But the important point is that even a small sample of migrants can be interesting provided it is taken daily.

In the United States radio masts take a considerable toll of nocturnal migrating birds but, though several workers have investigated the effects of power lines on low-flying bird migrants, I know of no one who has systematically collected dead birds from beneath these masts in Britain. Here is an opportunity for some enthusiast.

Holidays offer immense opportunities for research of any kind. School holidays, particularly in August and September, give a chance to get to grips with migrants. Bird observatories and well-known bird resorts are thronged with youngsters at this time, but other areas are totally neglected. Birds, including migrants, can be watched anywhere, but headlands and coastal sites can be discovered for yourself. Spend a few weeks at your own 'observatory' and reap the immense satisfaction that comes from discovering birds for yourself.

From being an observer of the birds that care to visit your garden it is not a vast step to becoming a passionate census worker or conservationist. The main thing is to remember that we are all interested in birds in our own different ways and for our own different purposes. Once you find yourself losing interest in birds – stop and think what you are parting with. Research is fine for those who enjoy it, duck counts for those who find pleasure in them, ringing for those who cherish the thrill of the hunt. But do not get involved in aspects of bird work that do not appeal to you. Try everything and stick to what you like doing best. And if that is just walking the countryside and watching common birds go about their everyday lives – that's fine. But please, don't condemn those who do not share your own approach, because they care, as you do, about the birds.

# Bibliography

The use of exhaustive bibliographies is a way of showing that authors have done their homework. What follows are my personal recommendations.

## Introductions to Birds

Fisher, James and Flegg, J. – *Watching Birds*, Poyser, 1974
Fisher, James and Peterson, Roger Tory – *World of Birds*, MacDonald, 1964
Fitter, R. S. R. – *Collins Guide to Bird-watching*, Collins, 1963
Huxley, Julian – *Bird-watching and Bird Behaviour*, Chatto and Windus, 1930
Smith, Stuart – *How to Study Birds*, Collins, 1945

## Identifying Birds

Brunn, Bertel *et al* – *The Hamlyn Guide to the Birds of Britain and Europe*, Hamlyn, 1970
Henzel, Herman *et al* – *The Birds of Britain and Europe*, Collins, 1972
Peterson, Roger Tory *et al* – *A Field Guide to the Birds of Britain and Europe*, Collins, 1954

## Background Data

Bannerman, D. A. – *The Birds of the British Isles*, Oliver & Boyd, 1953–63

British Ornithologists' Union – *The Status of Birds in Britain and Ireland*, Blackwell, 1971

Campbell, Bruce and Ferguson-Lees, James – *A Field Guide to Birds' Nests*, Constable, 1972

Cramp, Stanley *et al* – *The Seabirds of Britain and Ireland*, Collins, 1974

Fisher, James – *The Shell Bird Book*, Ebury Press and Michael Joseph, 1966

Gooders, John – *Where to Watch Birds*, Deutsch, 1967 and Pan Books, 1977

Gooders, John – *Where to Watch Birds in Europe*, Deutsch, 1970

Hollom, P. A. D. – *The Popular Handbook of British Birds*, Witherby, 1952

Witherby, H. F. *et al* – *The Handbook of British Birds*, 5 vols, Witherby, 1938–41

## Books for Enjoyment

Hosking, Eric and Lane, Frank – *An Eye for a Bird*, Hutchinson, 1970

Lack, David – *Enjoying Ornithology*, Methuen, 1965

Mountfort, Guy – *Portrait of a Wilderness*, Hutchinson, 1958

Mountfort, Guy – *Portrait of a River*, Hutchinson, 1962

Mountfort, Guy – *Portrait of a Desert*, Collins, 1965

Peterson, Roger Tory and Fisher, James – *Wild America*, Collins, 1956

Scott, Peter and Fisher, James – *A Thousand Geese*, Collins, 1953

Selous, Edmund – *Realities of Bird Life*, Constable, 1927

## Books on Specialities

Hosking, Eric and Gooders, John – *Wildlife Photography*, Hutchinson, 1973

Soper, Tony – *The New Bird Table Book*, David & Charles, 1973

## Journals

*Birds* – free to members of RSPB
*Bird Study* – free to members of BTO
*British Birds* – Macmillan Journals Ltd, 4, Little Essex Street, London, WC2R 3LF
*Ibis* – available to members of BOU
*World of Birds* – John Grant Publishing Ltd, 6, Queensthorpe Mews, Queensthorpe Road, London, SE26

# Index

Other Pan books that may interest you
are listed on the following pages

Tony Soper
**The New Bird Table Book** 60p

'If you are among those thousands of bird lovers who put out food for
your feathered visitors in winter, erect bird boxes in summer and try
to maintain a bird table all the year round – and then find that somehow
the birds don't come; here is the book for you . . .' THE DALESMAN
'Most comprehensive, containing everything that anyone could
possibly want to know on the subject' CAGE AND AVIARY BIRDS
'One of the best introductions to ornithology in a long time'
TEACHER'S WORLD

**The Complete Indoor Gardener** £3.95
Edited by Michael Wright
(Hardback edition £6.00)

The complete answer for everyone who loves growing plants but has
no garden. Whether you are a beginner or possess 'green fingers',
whether you live in a penthouse or a single room, these clear,
easy-to-follow instructions show how simple it is to grow all kinds of
plants both indoors and on patios and terraces, window ledges and
balconies, roof gardens and back yards. With 110 sections written by
fourteen specialist contributers, and over 600 illustrations, the
majority in colour, this is the ideal companion for the gardener without
a garden.

The book includes advice on : houseplants and indoor gardening ;
outdoor gardening without a garden ; dual-purpose plants ; exciting
special features ; and techniques and technicalities.

## Alan Young
### Sea Angling for Beginners 50p

Sea angling remains basically the problem of getting the fish to take a baited hook – by following the author's expert advice the new fisherman will avoid much disappointment. The book deals in a practical way with all the many aspects of fishing – what fish you may catch, what are the best baits to use, and there is a full coverage of tackle and techniques.

## Kenneth Seaman
### Canal Fishing 60p

Traditional methods and tackles are critically examined, and there is advice on bait selection and preparation. There are chapters on angling – for well-known species as well as the more unusual ones – match fishing techniques and the problems of canal maintenance.

## Trevor Housby
### Shark Fishing in British Waters 40p

Many varieties of shark may be found and fished within easy distance of Britain's coastline. Trevor Housby draws on a fund of shark-fishing expertise and experience to show how the use of light-tackle techniques and a sound knowledge of each individual species can place shark fishing at the top of the big-game fishing league, with its demands upon courage, endurance and skill.